ALL DAY IT IS MY CONVERSATION

Faith From the Depths of Kovno

RABBI ZALMAN ARYEH LEIB SCHAMES

&

SHAUL JOSHUA LENT

First published 2018

ISBN: 978-1-56871-650-3

Front Cover Picture: Rabbi Schames at granddaughter's award ceremony.

Back Cover Pictures, Left to Right: Nemun River, Rabbi Leib Schames' home (painted white) on Vaidoto Street, Vaidoto street sign.

Published by
Targum Publishers
Shlomo ben Yosef 131a/1
Jerusalem 9380581
editor@targumpublishers.com

For my mother and father

זאב מענדל בן שאול הלוי

חינה שרה בת הרב זלמן אריה ליב הלוי

Dedicated to my grandfather's family, his parents,
Yitzhak Meir and Chiene, and his siblings, Dov,
Avigdor, Yaacov David, Abba Tuvia, Rochel Devorah,
and Sarah Schames

Preface

At the end of August 2006 I informed my grandfather, Rabbi Leib Schames, that I intended to write a book about his life. I asked if he would be willing to share his story with me. He agreed to be interviewed, and we started in the beginning of September 2006.

In our first session, I collected introductory information about his childhood in Kovno, his education, and Jewish life in Lithuania.[1] The interview was productive and revealed much about life in pre-Holocaust Kovno. However, the next time I came to my grandfather's house, he informed me that he would not be able to continue. The interviews seemed to have reawakened old memories. Having a nightmare and feeling strained from the day before, he refused to proceed with the interviews.

My grandfather still wanted to complete the project. He felt it necessary to share his experience. Instead of continuing the interviews, my grandfather showed me some of his writings. He walked to his room and took out a tiny briefcase that sat on the bottom of a nightstand. The briefcase was filled with little slips of paper and a notebook. We both sat down, and he read one of his poems entitled "The Struggle of the *She'erith Hapleitah* [Leftover Remnant]." He read it, explaining the context and the purpose in writing such a poem. For the next few months, this process continued. He would pull out an essay and immediately began to say a few words. He would do this almost at random, retrieving some writing from his room and reviewing his words with me piece by piece. He asked midway through the essay, "Do you understand this?" or, "does this make sense?" I would nod, and he would finish his thought. My grandfather's writings were as diverse as they were meaningful. Many of these writings make up the central part of the book.

This book, entitled *All Day It Is My Conversation*, details the Jewish Holocaust in Kovno as well as my grandfather's memory and feelings of loss about the destroyed community of his childhood. My grandfather mostly wrote in Yiddish. Yiddish experts, therefore, were needed to translate his writtings into English. His October 1984 speech, "Dear Lithuanian Jews", was translated from Yiddish into English by Rabbi Shaul Seidler-Feller. Yiddish linguist and professor, Yakob Basner, translated all other Yiddish writings, including my grandfather's memoir. Following our agreement, Yakob transcribed the Yiddish part into a raw English. I have made some changes to the format and presentation to provide clarity. Any additions to the translation I have placed in brackets. The words in parenthesis were placed there by my grandfather.

The work transitions between a first and third person perspective. My grandfather's 1984 speech is presented initially. Following this I, in the third person, have provided a short introduction of Kovno Jewry and the community my grandfather was raised in. After describing life under Russian rule, I have placed my grandfather's first person memoir. His memoir is concise as it describes the early part of the Holocaust from the beginning of the German invasion in June 1941 until the decree to move into the ghetto on August 15, 1941. He wrote this memoir in the summer of 1947 in the small town of Bailly, and Paris, France.

My grandfather's experience, though, did not end in August 1941. He survived about three years in the Kovno ghetto and some nine months in the Kaufering Concentration Camp. I have therefore listened to interviews of my grandfather recorded by his son, Dr. Mayer Schames, recorded personal communications with my grandfather, reviewed other diaries, memoirs, oral testimonies, primary as well as secondary sources, and interviewed family members who knew about his experience, in order to complete his story.[2] These interviews are combined with some of my grandfather's own writings written immediately after his liberation and many years later. Interviews were conducted with Rabbi Leib Schames, Esther Schames, Dr. Mayer Schames, Dr. Joseph Schames, Dr. Warren Lent, Henny Lent (nee Schames), Rabbi Pinchas Gruman and fellow survivors of the Kovno Ghetto, Dr. Jack Brauns and Judith Meisel. I have done this in order to provide the reader with the complete story of my grandfather's experience in the Shoah, from his time in the ghetto until his liberation from Dachau-Kaufering.

The reader should note that the title from this book originated from a statement made by Rabbi Elazar Simcha Wasserman, the former Rosh Yeshivah of Ohr Elchonon – Jerusalem and Los Angeles. He characterized my grandfather using the verse in *Tehillim* 119:97, "How I love Your Torah, all day it is my conversation."[3]

My grandfather wrote in a very concise and straightforward manner. Like Rabbi Eliyahu of Vilna, the most famous Jew in Lithuania, the Gaon of Vilna, his words are simple and to the point. For the sake of simplicity, he sometimes left out the complexities of his argument and the halakhic background necessary to fully understand his message. To aid the reader yet not take anything away from my grandfather's actual words, I have provided background material, explanation, and sources in endnotes.

This work would not be possible without the help of several

individuals. My parents, Dr. Warren and Henny Lent, have constantly shown their support, from the initial stages of this work until its completion. They have provided encouragement, reviewed drafts, and provided advice about publication. I love you both. I hope that you continue to have *nachas* from our family. Rabbi Dr. Elijah Schochet consistently encouraged me throughout these years of writing. He has reviewed drafts, provided helpful suggestions, and has constantly shown an interest in the work. He has recommended books, provided source material, and introduced me to other scholars. His kindness to my grandfather and I has always been a *chesed shel emet*, a kindness with pure sincerity. My aunt, Faith Schames, has selflessly spent many hours reviewing the work, provided helpful suggestions, and is always willing to assist in any way. My brother and *chavrusa*, Andrew Lent, has consistently been willing to review portions of the work, provide sound advice as well as suggestions during the publication stages of this work. With his helpful interviews, my uncle, Dr. Mayer Schames, has allowed me to present my grandfather's story in full. My uncle, Dr. Joseph Schames, told me my grandfather's *chiddushei Torah* that were transmitted orally and gave me the ability to understand my grandfather's thought in its entirety. My grandmother, Mrs. Esther Schames, has always been willing to assist. With her warm personality, she has willingly answered questions and provided insight into her and her husband's life. My wonderful in-laws, Steven and Brigitte Lehat, have provided sound advice during the publication of the work. My sister-in-law, Sarah Lehat, designed the beautiful maps in this book and was always willing to help. Rabbi Nathan Kamenetsky reviewed an early draft and provided helpful suggestions. Thank you to my wife, Emmanuelle, and our children, Ahron and Leeba, who are my light. I love the three of you with all my heart. Finally, I thank G-d, the Giver of life, who has allowed me to participate in this work.

Thanks is also due to the following individuals who have reviewed sections of this work, provided useful information, warmly responded to emails, translated, and served as gracious interviewees. I am an independent researcher, without any ties to a scholarly organization, yeshivah or university. Yet, the following individuals have graciously responded to me, giving up their time to help: R. Akiva Atwood and the entire Targum staff, Dr. Alex Grobman, Alicia Brauns, R. Aryeh Striks, Avi and Daniella Schochet, Mr. and Mrs. Bowman, Ellis Raskin, R. Dr. Jeffery Woolf, R. Jeffrey Marx, Dr. Jack Brauns, Joyce Brauns, Judith Meisel, Manfred Kesting, R. Dr. Marc Shapiro, Menachem Kaiser, Michael Garber, Mina Cohen, Phyllis Lent, R. Pinchas Gruman, Ralph Codikow, Sanford Deutsch, Simon Goldberg, Shaul Ferraro, R. Shaul Seidler-Feller, Shulamith Berger, Yaakov Basner, and Yossi Marquis. It goes without saying that all opinions in this work are my grandfathers and my own.

* * *

My grandfather was a master of the Talmud and Tanach. Yet more than simply being a scholar, he practiced these words. He was someone who said each word of *kiddush* with enthusiasm, greeted everyone with a smile, and raised his children with decency. His actions followed his words and, as a result, the Torah that he said was all the more meaningful. His words here are few and concise, yet in all, I hope the content makes a lasting impression.

My Zeide was my Rebbe and role model. I know that for my siblings and cousins as well as aunts, uncles, and my parents this is a shared feeling. His children and grandchildren continue to speak about him. His stories and *divrei Torah* are spoken of as if he is still here. Just like the Torah of the Gaon was always on your lips, so too your Torah will always be on ours.

Shaul Lent
June 6, 2017
Los Angeles, California

Contents

LIST OF MAPS

Introduction

> How much has changed these last few years. My beginning was filled with pain. But now, almost suddenly, I have flourished. Nothing is missing in my life.[4] Thank G-d, I am alive and well, and my end is more blessed than my beginning.[5] This obligation, however, falls upon me. I must speak up. I must say a few words about an earlier generation. I must prepare myself for an investigation about our fathers.[6]

Dear Lithuanian Jews:

We are assembled here today to mark the memory of our precious fathers and mothers, brothers and sisters. Exactly forty-three years ago today, on the 28th of October, 1941, the *Grosse Aktion* of the Kovno Ghetto took place. Who among us can forget it? That terrible day, when the murderers, the Germans and Lithuanians, *yemach shemam*, tore away 12,000 Jews – men, women, and children – to shoot them at the Ninth Fort.

The Torah tells us about the tragedy of Aharon's two sons; they were burned by G-d. The Torah says, "*Va'yidom Aharon* – And Aharon was silent."[7] After such a tragedy, at a time that a father has to bury his children, Aharon became almost paralyzed; he was without words. The Torah states later on, "*V'acheichem Bnei Yisrael yibchu et haserefa asher saraf Hashem* – And their brothers, the House of Israel, should mourn over the fire which G-d burned."[8]

The Torah required *Bnei Yisrael* to mourn for just two Jewish children. Today, precious Jews, in that place, they led out 12,000 Jews – men, women, and children – undressed them completely and drove them into the pit. Fathers and mothers and children. The mothers had to watch the way they killed their children. In one moment, the past perished with the future. The blood of parents and children, bridegrooms and brides mixed together – a mixture of blood in one pit.

V'yibchu Bnei Yisrael et haserefa asher saraf Hashem – The Children of Israel should cry over the fire which Hashem burnt. Where does one get the words to express such a *churban* [destruction]? From where does one get the tears to mourn all of the thousands who perished in the *Grosse Aktion*? Where can one find the tears to cry for those who fell in all of the *Aktionen* – not just that of Kovno, but of all of the cities and villages of Lithuania; of the precious Jews who perished *al kiddush Hashem* [in sanctification of God's Name]? It is a tragedy that has never been equaled.

* * *

Leib finished his speech and walked back to his seat. "May you have strength," one survivor commented as he reached for his hand. "May you have continued strength," repeated another. There were a few praises, some pointed remarks. Leib sat down, confident and pained by his own words.

It has been thirty-two years since my grandfather, Rabbi Leib Schames, gave that speech and about ten years since he passed away. His speech has stopped, and his voice is no longer heard. His words, however, are still on my mind.

Kovno, the Pre-War Years

Kovno, Lithuania, 1930s

Right off the Nemun River, located not far from a small forest, stood the Schames's home. It looked just like a store. A brick building, the facade was painted white standing without a proper entryway. A few inches of grass made up the front yard. Walking through the driveway, however, the atmosphere seemed to change. The side of the house curved where purple and orange flowers, as well as other greenery, lined a walkway towards the back door.

Among the beautiful atmosphere of river and forest, among the small wooden home and the barn which seamlessly attached itself to the main house, stood Chiene. She did everything in that little home. Selling flour and grains in front, she traded with local Lithuanian military men stationed a few blocks down the road. Chiene alternated between her work as a merchant and her duty as a mother. When the older children, Leib and his younger siblings, Dov and Rochel, returned home from school, the children, seven in all, seemed to converge on her as she multitasked between closing shop and cooking dinner.[9]

The house bustled like a little marketplace. Yet Chiene bore her lot with grace. She loved her husband, Yitzhak Meir, who learned Talmud at the local House of Study. She loved her children. Day in, she labored in the flour and grain store, sustaining the family and finding comfort in the warmth of her home.[10]

* * *

> *You must see the yeshivah students in Kovno, the glorious bachurim who struggle for the sake of Torah. They do not rest from their studies. They emulate the deeds of their teachers, constantly striving in the ocean of Torah and listening to the words of the greats among them.*[11]

It was not Kovno's ornate architecture or abundant tourist sites that attracted the eye. The land overlooking the Nemun river looked beautiful. But for the most part, the houses in Kovno were run down and dilapidated. Many people, especially in the suburb of Slobodka, lived in poverty. Some 32,000 Jewish residents bought and sold small goods in the marketplace. Families crammed into small, decrepit wooden homes which lacked running water. The area stood out in one respect – the Slobodka Yeshivah stood in Kovno.

The Jewish community in Kovno idealized religious learning and viewed the Slobodka Yeshivah as the jewel of the city. This was true for Leib's town as well. Living in a suburb of Kovno called Panemune, Leib's life revolved around the Slobodka Yeshivah. In the winter, the Nemun River would freeze, and Leib would cross the bridge to make it in time for morning prayers. In the spring, the Vilya River and the connecting Nemun would overflow and destroy the Slobodka bridge. During this time, Leib would cross by boat to get to the yeshivah.[12] Leib had blue eyes and black hair. He was a mischievous boy, often playing games with his best friend, Nathan Codikow, around the Panemune forest. He was a husky kid, strong enough to swim back and forth across the Nemun

River.[13] Yet, everything always came back to the yeshivah. His parents were constantly encouraging him. His mother, especially, would carefully monitor his studies, often crossing the Panemune bridge to see how Leib and Dov were progressing in their learning.[14]

* * *

The student body at the Slobodka Yeshivah was incredibly large. In the beginning of the twentieth century, enrollment at the yeshivah grew to over four hundred students.[15] From its *yeshivah ketanas* [schools for younger boys], *Ohr Yisrael* and *Ohel Moshe*, to its college of higher learning, *Knesset Yisrael*, the student body at the Slobokda Yeshivah increased to an incredible extent. Boys came from around the world to attend the yeshivah.

More than its size, though, the Slobodka Yeshivah was known as the first yeshivah to combine intensive Talmudic learning with a strong emphasis on character development and conscious devotion to G-d called *mussar*.[16] Most of the students possessed a strong work ethic and learned Talmud for many hours.[17] "We must always improve," explained the Slobodka Yeshivah founder, Rabbi Nathan Tzvi Finkel, "never still, never ceasing to reach for even higher heights."[18] "If I knew that I would only reach this level," he preached, "I would not be able to live with myself; but if I did not strive to be like Rabbi Elijah, the famed genius of Vilna, the greatest Talmudic Sage known throughout Lithuania, then I would not have even reached this level."[19]

At the same time that the Slobodka Yeshivah student devoted themselves to intensive Talmudic learning, the students put a strong emphasis on ethical *mussar* lessons. They studied books that inspired conscious devotion to G-d and contained a moral message. Yeshivah teachers taught students to make decisions based on logic rather than emotions. They emphasized the idea that man was created in the Divine image and therefore should dress and act with dignity and self-respect. They aspired to such traits as greeting everyone cheerfully, performing the commandments with alacrity and order, behaving mindfully, keeping one's word, maximizing one's time in study, and showing kindness to others.[20]

For many, even the more secular, the Slobodka Yeshivah was regarded as the country's gem, a Lithuanian treasure, serving as a bastion for intelligent, religious students from around the world. Lithuanian Jews recognized the Slobodka Yeshivah as a place of scholarship. They looked with admiration at those chosen few who could devote themselves to full-time Talmud study. Even more, people recognized the Slobodka Yeshivah as a breeding ground for Jewish leadership, both lay and religious. Well known doctors and academics, as well as Rabbis and religious lay leaders, could be counted among its alumni.[21] And the more leaders the school produced, the more the Slobodka Yeshivah's reputation grew.

* * *

Like any traditional society confronting modernity, Jews in Kovno maintained their traditions to varying degrees. Some became socialists, communists, yiddishists, and zionists. Others became indifferent to religion, emigrating to the United States and elsewhere to find employment and financial stability. Leib, however, continued to remain influenced by the traditional-religious world of the yeshivah. At a very young age, Leib's parents sent him to *cheder*, where he learned elementary Hebrew and Bible, and then the Slobodka Yeshivah and its school for younger boys called *Ohel Moshe*. Studying under a *Rosh Yeshivah* named Rabbi Yosef Chaim Zaks (1879-1941), he devoted the majority of his time to the study of the Talmud. Leib learned in the Slobodka Yeshivah with great exuberance. His power of recall was strong for his age, and he memorized certain portions of the Talmud by heart.[22] Though aware of the intellectual and cultural trends of his time, for Leib, Torah and tradition played the most important role in his early life.[23]

* * *

The Jews of Lithuania maintained a culture of their own, unique in comparison to the surrounding population. Many possessed a strong Jewish identity and few considered assimilation, since an extensive barrier existed between Jews and gentiles. As opposed to Lithuanian gentiles who were mostly farmers, Lithuanian Jews were often merchants and storekeepers.[24] Some Jews spoke Hebrew, Russian and German. All knew and spoke Yiddish, and only rarely, though increasingly after the First World War, did they converse in Lithuanian.[25]

Distinguishable in dress, mannerisms, culture, and language, Lithuanian gentiles looked upon Jews as foreigners. They were always known to be different and stigmatized as such, but in the 1920's this difference took on racialist form. At the end of the First World War, politicians and peasants openly referred to the Jews as thieves and swindlers. The market is brimming with Jews, they claimed.[26] By late 1933, anti-Semitism had been so rampant that the once tolerant President of Lithuania, Antanas Smetona, openly described the Jews as corrupt merchants and closet communists.[27] He was not alone in this respect, and by the mid-1920's, Lithuanian state officials restricted Jews from working on Sunday, ensured that Jews did not hold government positions, and restricted Jews from many liberal professions.[28]

In many cases, anti-Semitic sentiments were linked with the growing Lithuanian nationalist movement. While Leib was a young child, signs began to appear in Lithuania such as "Lithuania only for Lithuanians" or "There is no place for outsiders."[29] These slogans excluded all minority groups and specifically Jews. Anti-Semitism came from all walks of life. They were young and old, Catholics and politically active Lithuanians. Ardently anti-communist and committed to the newly formed independent state, these men and women idealized the country and advocated for a totalitarian, pure country, free from foreign influences.[30]

ON JUNE 15, 1940

The Russian–Communist government invaded independent Lithuania. Within a few months, the communists destroyed the Lithuanian army and dismantled all private industries. They nationalized banks, industrial plants, and larger shops. Social and financial organizations transferred to the public sector and the new government forced all political parties, except for the Communist party, to close. Jewish life dissipated as well. The Russians disbanded many of the yeshivas, burned Jewish books, and created laws which forced Jews to work on Shabbat and other religious holidays.[31] Though many Jews continued to practice Judaism secretly, within the year, the Russians destroyed much of Lithuania's once vibrant Jewish life.[32]

Many Jews feared the communists. The government sent communal leaders to Siberia and contributed to the community's financial decline. They decimated Jewish culture and uprooted any hope of returning to their old status as an autonomous minority. However, despite these enactments, the Russians considered gentiles and Jews to be politically equal. As they viewed all religion to be evil, the Communists did not discriminate against Jews any more than they did Christians. Additionally, the Russian government allowed Jews to work in several sectors of the economy in which they were previously barred. Some Jews used their newfound freedom to work for the communist regime directly. Others managed government corporations and participated in the judiciary and the military.[33]

Most Lithuanian gentiles looked at this phenomenon with disgust. Before communism, Lithuania had been an independent country. Now Jews aided the very forces that destroyed their culture, government, and community. They believed Jews to be treacherous, abandoning their country in a time of subjugation. This was a gross misrepresentation. Most Jews also despised the new government, viewing communism as only a little better than

Nazism.[34] However, some Jews did aid the Russian government and, as a result, many Lithuanians perceived the Jewish community to be linked with the Communist party. Years later, Leib stated, "Since Jewish people helped the communist government, they paid a very high price."[35] This price would be paid in blood.

June 1941

The German army moved closer to Lithuania. As Germany marched towards the border, Jews gathered around consulates, pleading with foreign officials to procure exit visas. The Japanese Embassy, under the leadership of Sempo Sugihara, produced emigration papers for thousands of Jews for a small price of two litas.[36] Yet, most foreign governments placed limitations on those who could enter their country. Most were forced to remain in Lithuania.

On June 22, 1941, the German air force dropped bombs on Kovno's airport in the suburb of Alexot.[37] The Russian army ran. In their place, Lithuanian fascists attacked the Jewish community.

The German Invasion

The following is a translation of my grandfather's autobiographical memoir about his experience during the first months of the German occupation in 1941. He wrote these words about two years after his liberation from Dachau-Kaufering, in June 1947, while living in France. His words have been translated from the original Yiddish.

June 22 – 24, 1941

It was summer, early in the morning. While everyone was still asleep, fresh air from the Lithuanian fields and woods blew through the open windows. Suddenly, bomb explosions and cannon firings awoke us. The explosions were so massive that the window frames fell out. It was 3 a.m., Sunday, June 22nd, 1941. I thought that the raucous was Red Army drills. We all went back to sleep. We were dreaming of our plans for the upcoming day and running errands. When I got up at 6 a.m. and turned on the radio, I heard the wild voice of that bandit Hitler. He announced that he had attacked the Soviet Union, the "Jewish Communists."

I ran outside and saw the Kovno airport burning. Coal and black smoke rose up to the sky. It was burning from the bombardment at 3:00 a.m. Around 8:30 a.m., I heard Molotov [the Soviet Union's Minister of Foreign Affairs] on the Moscow radio announcing that German bandits unexpectedly attacked the Soviet Union. Afterward, at around 12:00 noon, we heard the news that the Germans had crossed the border and were already twenty kilometers into Lithuanian territory. Not knowing what to do, the Jews ran around confused. Should they run to the train or rent a carriage and head on the road to Russia? Sunday night, my father, *alav hashalom* [may he rest in peace], decided to hire carriages and start in the direction of Vilna, Russia.[38]

The next morning, Monday, June 23rd, the Russians blew up the bridges that connected Kovno with the rest of the province. These actions did not hinder us. We loaded only essential necessities on the wagon and left the entire house unattended. Our family began the journey. At noon, we left Kovno–Panemune. We took side roads since troops of fleeing Russian soldiers had taken the main roads. During the trip, we experienced several attacks by German airplanes. They shot at us with machine guns, but luckily the Germans did not hit anyone. We continued on the same path until late in the evening. Afterward, we spent the night with a Lithuanian peasant.

Early the next morning, we started on the road again. Our family did not get far that Tuesday. The German tanks were faster than us. We met them forty kilometers before Vilna, which meant that the Germans were in Vilna before they got to Kovno. They came through Grodna and occupied Vilna before entering Kovno. The escaping Jews, all of us, were left in the paws of the Germans. When my father saw the first German, he announced that all was now lost. Only G-d should help us!

We turned around to go back. Some peasants we knew told us that if a German saw a Jew on the road, they would shoot him (and take everything away). Father hired one of the peasants to accompany us until we got back to Kovno–Panemune. On the road, we encountered many fascists with large amounts of weapons. Luckily these Lithuanian fascists were acquaintances of ours, and they let us through. We passed a small forest five hundred meters away from where the Lithuanian fascists encamped. We could see, already, many Jewish bodies murdered in the woods and recognized some of the dead. It was surely the work of the Lithuanian fascists.

The Slobodka Pogrom

If only my head were water and my eyes a spring of tears so that I could cry day and night for the slain of my people.
- Yirmeyahu 8:23

It was the end of June

I was in the city again. I did not see any Jews in the streets. Lithuanian fascists, with white armbands and rifles on their shoulders, were everywhere. They were all gentile bandits from our little town of Panemune. The next day, Wednesday, the 25th of June, we heard the terrible news that a large pogrom had taken place in Slobodka. Lithuanian fascists, hooligans, had broken into Jewish houses and slashed, stabbed, and robbed the Jewish inhabitants. Their victims were both young and old Jews. Among them was the Slobodka Rabbi, Rav Zalman Osowsky.[39] With a saw, they cut off his head and placed it in the window. They then threw his body into a garbage can. The Lithuanian fascists took men and women, with infants in their arms, to the Slobodka Bridge and forced them to dig a grave. After having been fiercely beaten, the poor people reluctantly dug the grave for half of the day. At approximately 2:00 p.m., the shooting began. The criminals shot women, with infants in their arms, and buried them half alive. They pierced the children with bayonets and threw them, still breathing, into the mass grave. Six young men were left. They were allowed to live temporarily to bury the dead. After they had finished their job, they threw these gravediggers into the Vilya [River] and drowned them.

The day after the pogrom, I traveled to Slobodka. I entered a house where a wife, a husband and three children lay in a river of their own blood; the [Lithuanians] had stabbed them with knives. I entered another room and saw an old, white-haired man lying on the floor. He had also been stabbed. He lay near a white wall, his stomach completely open and his intestines spilled out. His fingers were soiled in blood. I saw on a wall closest to him, written in blood, the word "*nekamah* [revenge]."

On the following day, the 26th of June, somebody knocked on the door. I opened the door and saw a group of Lithuanian fascists who ordered us to get dressed and follow them. So, with rifles in their hands, they took my father, my little brother, and I. Father asked them where they were taking us; their answer: "You've lived long enough, we will take care of you." The fascists took us to the place where all Panemune Jews gathered [the Flack artillery building]. They tightly guarded the area. We remained in the [building] for three days.[40] On the third day, a Lithuanian fascist came with an official paper in his hand. He began to read different names. They divided us into two groups: one group they released, the other, which consisted of the greatest leaders of the little town, including the Rabbi of Panemune, Rabbi Yeffeh, they detained. They read a document stating that we, the arrested ones, were suspected of being communists and of collaborating with the Russians. The Lithuanian fascists then ordered us to line up in a row. Carefully guarding us, the Lithuanians took us in the direction of the Sixth Fort. On the way, a Rabbi said *vidui* [the prayer of repentance said before death]. He would say the prayer and we would repeat the words after him.

We arrived at the Sixth Fort. Located not far from Petrushin, the Fort had been built by Nicholas of Russia to defend Kovno from the left wing. The Fort consisted of a fortress surrounded by strong, thick walls. The Fort looked as though it had been built from one piece of concrete. The walls were three floors high and two or three meters thick. The entry to the Fort, though, was located about ten meters underground. The yard was like a valley or a grave with high concrete walls surrounding it. The bandits chose such forts as the best slaughterhouses since nobody could see or hear anything and no one could escape.

At the Fort, we saw Germans stationed by machine guns. Not far from the guns, German soldiers were standing and digging graves. Suddenly, buses arrived filled with Russian Jews and Red-Army soldiers. The [Germans] chased them from the buses, beat them with sticks and [struck them] against the head. A German officer then blew his whistle. Guards ran alongside the trenches and began to shoot at the Russian Jews with their machine guns. All of them fell to the ground. Many were wounded. Half alive, they lay there moaning and screaming. A second whistle was then blown. The German soldiers left the trenches and began to throw those shot and wounded, who were still alive, into the graves. They poured white lime over them and buried their victims.

After witnessing this horrible spectacle, a tall, fat German came and asked the Lithuanian fascists why they had brought us here. The fascists took out a paper written half in Lithuanian, half in German and read out loud that we were suspected communists. "Yes," said the German, "in five minutes all of them will be finished." My father took the initiative, "We are not communists," he retorted, "we are innocent people." "Yes," replied the German, "the people must be investigated." So instead of remaining there, the [fascists] took us to the Lithuanian police station for interrogation.

The Sixth Fort was five kilometers from Kovno. On the

way to the Lithuanian police, bandits traveled on the road. The Lithuanians asked them if they would like to have our clothes. "Why not?" answered the bandits. "But on one condition," responded the fascists, "you should not spare hitting them." The bandits took us to a small forest, undressed us completely and began battering us with sticks. They took away our clothes and gave us their rags. After we had put them on, they took us to the police, the "*Sauguma*."

Already five hundred Jews stood in the yard who had been captured on the street. They informed us that they had been at the "*Sauguma*" station for two days. Nobody interrogated them. They were beaten to death and tortured. We demanded to be investigated. "It does not matter if you are a Communist or a Democrat," the police answered, "all Jews must die." At 8:00 p.m., Germans came to observe the Jews and play with them a little. They picked up the Rabbi of Panemune, Rabbi Yeffeh, and [tortured this] old man. The Germans ripped out half of his white and gray beard and made him walk on the streets with a half-plucked beard. Under arrest, we remained in the "*Sauguma*" station for three days.

On the third day, in the evening, Germans arrived and took fifteen people to work. In the three day period that I was there, they had arrested 2,000 Jewish Kovno men. They captured them on the streets or took them from their homes. For three days, we remained there without anything to eat. There was only some water to drink. On the fourth day, early in the morning, the German Gestapo arrived. It was the first time I saw them, these "*malechei chavalah* [angels of destruction]." Outside, on the entire street near the police station, stood many parked buses. They ordered us to enter the vehicles, thirty people to a bus. Under the guard of the Lithuanian fascists, the [Gestapo] took us to the Seventh Fort.

The Seventh Fort

Anti-Semitism increased as soon as the Germans arrived. Wherever a Lithuanian fascist met a Jew, whether on a street or on the way back to Kovno, with one word the Lithuanian took them to the Seventh Fort. The Seventh Fort looked exactly like the Sixth Fort and was located three kilometers from Kovno on a green hill. Our captors used the Seventh Forth from the 29th of Sivan 5700 [July 5, 1940] until the 12th of Tammuz 5701 [July 7, 1941]. The Lithuanian police, the "*Sauguma*", took us to the Seventh Fort during the hottest time of the year. Under the open sky, they chased 8,000 Jews together to the yard of the Fort. Although the place could only hold 2,000 people, they pressed 8,000 Jews together under the burning hot sun.

From eight in the evening until six the next morning, the people had to lie quietly without moving. We lay there stacked, eight people, one on top of the other. When someone made a move, even the slightest twitch, the enemy immediately fired their guns. With only one shot they could kill three or four people. They used dum-dum bullets, which would explode on impact. When a bullet hit someone's hand, there would be nothing left to the individual's hand. If they hit someone's head, the [skull] completely tore open.

Pressed together, one on top of the other, it was impossible to lie at night and not move. When someone did, the Germans began to shoot. During these nights, they killed eighty or ninety people in this manner. Besides death from a gunshot wound, tens of people lay smothered in a cramped area and suffocated. In all, they murdered eighty to a hundred people every night. Additionally, every evening, from eight to nine, they took Jews in groups of fifty and told them that they were peeling potatoes. Instead, they took them out to be shot. One at a time, they assembled five groups of fifty. No one would return. The same procedure repeated in the morning. This second phase of shooting started at five in the morning and lasted an hour. In this way, the Nazis killed around five hundred Jews every day.

Lithuanian young fascists, called the *Jauna Lietuva*, would come to us to learn how to shoot. They would stand up on the bunker, about one hundred meters away, and fire into the crowd. The dead among us would later be taken away to a little hill.

Once, I also had to take away the dead. A group of us carried bodies to a small hill where a huge grave, the size of a large pit, had been prepared. Barrels filled with carbolic lime and shovels lay by the hole. There was a lot of blood around the pit, enough to make mud. When we came close to the hole, we saw those people taken each morning and evening. They had been shot in this area and placed in the pit like herring. One on top of the other, they were doused with lime and a thin layer of earth. The following day, the process repeated. In such a way, 8,000 Jews were shot and, in the same pit, buried together.[41] After the corpses had been brought, we buried and poured lime over them. Following this, they took us back to the group.

It was so hot during the month of Tammuz. We were pressed together one on top of the other. Yet what did they give us to eat? They gave us salted fish and a small amount of water. Everyone was thirsty from the intense heat and even more so from the salty fish. Then, while distributing the water, they began to shoot at us. When our tormentors came with water, everyone tried to grab it. Jews sought to satisfy their thirst with this small amount of water. However, as soon as the people began to extend their hands, the Lithuanians, with machine guns, opened fire on the thirsty crowd. Tens of people died from dehydration. Their deaths robbed the Lithuanian bandits of the opportunity to shoot at them and excuse their acts by claiming that the Jews disobeyed orders. There were many loopholes to torture Jews in sadistic ways.

In the Fort, there was a section organized for women as well. The women's camp was located in wet, dark bunkers near the Fort. On the second day at the Fort, my mother brought food for father, *alav hashalom* [may peace be upon him], my brother, *alav hashalom*, and I. She brought a basket with sugar, butter, and other foods. The Lithuanian ruffians let her in, but they did not let her out. They confined her in the bunker together with other Jewish women who had brought the men food. Father shared our food with others.

On the Third Day at the Seventh Fort

A Lithuanian fascist came looking for Doctor Shochad. Not knowing what would soon happen to him, the doctor followed orders and came forward. The fascist removed him from the crowd and shot him with a machine gun in both legs. As he fell to the ground in terrible pain, Doctor Shochad began to shout and beg the fascist to kill him. Instead, one fascist took out a pistol and shot the doctor's hand. The wounded doctor lay in a river of his blood and again asked the fascist to put him out of his misery and shoot him in the head or the heart. "It will not be easy for you to die," said the fascist, "we will torture you and then you will die." So, the fascist shot him in the hands and legs again until the doctor shouted, "Repent Jews; *Shema Yisrael Adoni Eloheinu Adoni Echad* [Hear Israel, Hashem is our G-d, Hashem is One]."

These were Doctor Shochad's last words. They were also the last words from all the Jews. Like this, thousands of Jews were tortured and victimized without mercy.

I knew a fascist in the Seventh Fort who had seen all of the shootings and the torture. He approached me and pleaded that he was not guilty of these crimes and was forced by his comrades to be on guard. He told me that he could not look at the things going on in front of him and could not witness the barbaric torture of people. Once, standing at his post, he threw away his rifle, tore his hair and began to scream, "What are you doing to these people?" A comrade of his ran by and shot him. It was documented later that the fascist had a mental breakdown after witnessing such acts of torture.

The prisoners hoped that the end would come as soon as possible. We all wished that a bullet would find us, or a German airplane would fly over our head. Many times, I begged the Almighty to let them bomb us. That would be the end. We already experienced so much.

The fourth day at the Seventh Fort

We remained on the ground at night, one on top of the other. With four men on top of me, the [Lithuanian] partisans shot their bullets. This was nothing new to me. Close by, I heard Jews moaning. The stray bullets had wounded them. Suddenly, I felt a hot sensation on my neck. When I touched my back, I felt fluid, and I immediately understood that it was blood. I was sure that I had been shot. I did not feel any pain. It seemed like it was a very easy thing to die. If this is what death felt like, it was a good thing that a bullet hit me. In the morning, though, when we were allowed to stand up, I realized that this whole dream of my death was false. Instead of dying, the person lying on top of me died, and it was his blood that leaked on my neck. By that point, I was so soaked that when I ultimately left the Fort, the foul smell of blood still permeated my clothing. They continued to smother and shoot at us every day. Four thousand Jews remained.

ON THE FIFTH DAY, IN THE EVENING

The barbarian fascists entered the bunkers where the women stayed. They ordered all girls aged eighteen to twenty to report voluntarily for work. Nobody wanted to go. The women knew where the bandit-fascists would take them. Commotion erupted. Using spotlights, the fascists ran around and looked into each girl's face. They showed interest in one woman and took her. They desired another girl and grabbed her. In some cases, they violently took fourteen and fifteen-year-old girls from their mother's arms. In all, the Lithuanians kidnapped forty-three Jewish women. The girls cried, the mothers cried. They pulled out their hair; nothing helped. "Goodbye Mother," the young girls screamed, "I will never see you again." After forcing the girls to line up in a row, the fascists took the girls to the pits where the men had been murdered and ordered them to undress. The girls refused. The fascists started to rip off their clothing. The girls fought, they resisted fiercely. However, they could not overpower the fascists. The Lithuanians tied the girls to the trees, raped and shot them.

ON THE SIXTH DAY

A group of the bandits came and announced that whoever had money, gold, or watches must hand them over. Since no one wanted to give up these goods, people began to throw their valuables randomly on the ground. The Lithuanian fascists then [ordered] those who had a leather coat, a decent suit or a suitable pair of boots to remove them. Whoever did not take their boots or suit off fast enough was beaten to death. The people were already weak from the daily, constant suffering as well as the starvation rations. Soon, they would not have to shoot anymore. The Jews looked lifeless. We were decimated. Out of the 8,000 people that came to the Fort, only 1,500 people remained.

ON THE TWELFTH DAY, IN THE EVENING

My father lay still. I rested on his right side and my little brother on his left. Suddenly, I heard father begin to moan. "Father, what happened?" I asked. "Children, I am wounded," he said, "a bullet hit me." When I heard his words, I stood up and took my father out of the crowd so he would not have to lie on the others. I began to take off his clothes. When I reached his *tallis katan* [religious undergarment] I realized that it was covered completely in blood. "This is Torah and this is its reward," I said to him. He said that I should be quiet since a person is not allowed to speak that way. His words rang in my ears, exactly as the prayer for the *harugei malchut,* the Yom Kippur prayer commemorating the ten Jewish martyrs killed at the hands of the Romans: "If I hear another sound, I will turn the entire universe to water!"* I removed his *tallis katan* and saw his mutilated arm. Immediately, I tried to look for a doctor to place a bandage on him.

This all took place when prisoners were forced to lie still and not move. When the bandits saw that I was searching the area to find a bandage, they began to shoot at me. I did not pay attention to the bullets around me. I did not want to see my father die from his wound. The bandits continued firing their weapons. The bullets seemed to whistle around me. The bandits murdered other Jews nearby, but they did not want to kill me. I realized that they wanted me to stand and move around as long as possible to give

---

* Yom Kippur *Mussaf, Eleh Ezkera* prayer, in the section discussing Rabbi Yishmael's martyrdom: "The celestial angels bitterly cried, 'This is Torah and this is its reward. G-d, who wraps Himself in light like a garment, the enemy insults Your great and awesome Name. They disparage and blaspheme against your words.' A voice from Heaven responded, 'If I hear another sound, I will turn the universe to water. I will turn the world to astonishing emptiness. This is the decree before Me; accept it, you who rejoice in the Torah.' "

them the chance to kill others. The people begged me to have pity on them and lie down. They knew that the Lithuanians would continue to fire their guns until all of them were killed. Father told me a passage from *Chazal* [our Sages] in which the Talmud states, "Even if a knife rests upon your neck do not give up, the Master of the World will have mercy."[42] Father then told me to lie down, "Bandits are shooting when you stand near me." I crept down and gave my coat to father so that he could cover himself. I then thought about what I would do next. Father was severely wounded and would soon pass from this world. I still did not want to believe it.

I knew that if I stayed here, I would not survive either. It came to my mind that maybe it was best if I ran away. However, I knew that if I tried to escape, they would shoot and kill me. On the other hand, if I ran, I would not have to witness the death of my father and brother. Maybe it was better to be killed earlier and not suffer to such an extent. While trying to figure everything out, I felt my brother move closer to me and lay on my legs. He fell quietly asleep. I lay there silently until the signs of morning appeared.

It was the 12th of Tammuz [July 7, 1941]

This morning was somehow different from all the others. There were a lot of machine guns. Many Lithuanian fascists arrived at the Fort. I did not like any of it. I woke up my little brother. "Be prepared," I said to him, "all of us will be murdered soon." We said *vidui* and waited. I heard one of the older fascists call out loudly,

> "The Jews who served voluntarily in the Lithuanian army in the year 1920, who fought against the Bolsheviks, must stand up and go to one side. If a stranger stands up, he will be shot immediately. You will be taken to the Yellow Prison for interrogation."

Around thirty Jews were taken from the Fort to the Yellow

Prison. (They were murdered two months later.) After a few minutes, there was another announcement: "Children up to fourteen years old must go to their mothers." At the time, I was fifteen years old.[43] I told my brother, who was thirteen, to run in the direction where the fascists stood. He was busy gathering children who were younger than fourteen years old. Afterward, my little brother left. I remained in my place and did not make any movement. Suddenly, I heard my father begin to moan. "Run, my child, and save yourself," he told me forcefully. I kissed him, and with tears in my eyes, I began to run.

Although I was only fifteen, I looked like an eighteen-year-old. As a result, when the bandits saw that I was running, they started to shoot at me. Like an experienced soldier, I continuously ran and ducked. The bullets whistled passed my ears. I fell and lay on the ground for a minute, watching as the bullets exploded ten centimeters away from me. When they stopped to reload, I stood up again and ran a second time. I then reached a Lithuanian fascist and showed him the papers that proved that I was fifteen years old.[44] At last, he let me go to the women's side.

Some Lithuanian fascists placed me in a group of twenty-five children and took us all to the women. Though I was safe at that point, those who remained behind, in the men's area, were not as fortunate. As we left the crowd, the fascists fired their machine guns at the crowd of men. After about fifteen minutes, they stopped.

The Lithuanians brought us to the bunkers where the women slept. As soon as we arrived, the women asked us about the intensive shooting. I did not want to make anyone panic, so I told them that it was a drill to check their ammunition. After the shooting ceased, I could see the guards leaving the area and singing one of their songs. I understood then that every person must have been killed. I ran around looking for my mother and asked some acquaintances if they knew where she was. They told me that she was in room number fourteen. I went to the room and saw her. Mother did not recognize me. I had changed completely during the nineteen [sic] days that I spent in the Fort. I looked so terrible that my own mother could not identify me. Mother started to ask me about father. I began to cry and told her the whole truth.[45]

An hour after the shooting had stopped, the [fascists] chased the women from the bunkers and ordered them to line up in a row. The Lithuanian fascists took them all to the Ninth Fort. The sick and the weak were taken by car while the rest were forced to walk by foot, for twelve kilometers, from the Seventh Fort to the Ninth Fort. Leaving the fort, I could see a bus arriving with the greatest Rabbis from Slobodka. Among them, I recognized my Rosh Yeshivah, Rabbi Yosef Chaim Zaks, *zt'l.* With one of the Rabbis holding a red flag, the fascists took the leaders through the city to prove to the people that all Rabbis are communists.[46] The Lithuanian fascist tossed the group from the bus like calves. They beat them with sticks. When we came closer, the fascists ordered the Rabbis to turn their faces towards the wall.

The Lithuanians brought women together with children to the Ninth Fort. On the way, I could have eluded the guards and escaped. But I chose to stay with the group. I had run from my father to my mother. There was nowhere to run to if I left my mother. If we had to die, let it be together. We arrived at the Ninth Fort.

On the next day, the 13th of Tammuz [July 8, 1941]

Twenty children, including me, were taken to work. The [Lithuanian fascists] took us back to the Seventh Fort towards the area where the prisoners were previously stationed. No one was there this time. The entire place had been covered with carbolic lime. We understood that not one person [who stayed in the men's area] survived. Forced by the Lithuanians, we loaded fiftykilogram kegs, filled with carbolic lime, into a car. The job was burdensome. All of us were fatigued from the journey. The group consisted of children, mind you. Large Lithuanian bandits stood nearby with sticks in their hands and smacked the little children's faces. We loaded the material onto a big car and took the kegs to the Ninth Fort.

When we returned to the women, we told them what we saw at the Seventh Fort and what was happening. Immediately, the women began to cry and panic. With small children in their hands, they ran around their cells and screamed. Their voices reached the heavens themselves. Our captors promised us that they would release us.

We could not trust their words. If they were going to free us, we said, they should do it now. An old fascist came to the prisoners in the evening and promised us that we would be released in the morning. Early the next day, a taxi arrived with members of the Gestapo. They considered the situation. The women, filled with fear, continued to scream and pull their hair. Finally, after a few minutes of deliberation, one of the older leaders of Gestapo said, "Let them go, we can find this garbage any time we need to." They did not let us leave, though. As soon as the Germans came to the fort, they kicked and beat the women. They pulled children away from their mother's arms and threw them to ground. But the children did not cry anymore. They no longer screamed the word, "Mother."

On the next day, the 14th of Tammuz [July 9, 1941]

They began to release us. Mothers with infants were the first to be freed. After that, they released everyone else. One after the other, they let another group of fifty women [and children] leave. By the evening, nobody remained in the Ninth Fort. As I was leaving the Fort, a Lithuanian fascist told me that they only released us because they did not prepare graves and digging them would take some time. They did not want to keep the women and children together for those hours. "Anytime we need you, we will find you," said the fascist, "you will not evade us."

After our release, my mother, brother and I returned to our home. We saw my little brothers and sisters. Every day gentiles came to our house and claimed to have pity on us. In truth, though, they came to take our possessions. These bandits pretended to sympathize with us, but [once they entered our home,] they stole our goods. At that point, when I returned home, I felt that I was responsible for the entire family. I was the oldest of five boys and two girls. This whole burden stood on my shoulders. I became extremely pensive and no longer had the desire to play pranks. I was astonished at how my neighborhood friends, who were the same age as me, ran around and had fun as though nothing had happened and nothing had changed. Troubles that impacted every Jewish family and those that affected my own family specifically weighed heavily on my mind.

* * *

As soon as a Lithuanian fascist recognized the face of a Jew, he would arrest him. The Lithuanians would go to different Jewish homes and steal from them. They incarcerated the Jews strategically. They made them believe that they had come to arrest them and that if the residents wanted to remain alive, they would have to give up their money and gold. After the Jews had given them their money, the fascists arrested the men and took them to work.

There were a lot of Jewish and Russian bodies on the roads. The dead remained in the heat for an extended period of time. A terrible smell came from these corpses. The [Lithuanian fascists] forced only the Jews to do the dirty job of burying the dead. They would order the Jews to dig a grave a little bigger than required and told them, "Make a place for yourself as well because, after work, we will kill you too." In many cases, they were not lying.

Lithuanian fascists grabbed forty Jewish men and brought them to an area known as the Young Postures Prospect. The fascists brought them to a garage and started to torture and abuse the men. They forced the Jews to clean the garage as fast as possible. They expected them to labor at an incredible speed. But, whatever the Jews did, they could not work faster than a machine. The Lithuanians started to beat the Jewish laborers. After work had finished, they closed the garage with the people inside. They took hoses with water and iron bars. Twenty bandits, with the iron bars and car springs in their hands, started striking the Jews. Those who received a blow stayed on the ground. The fascists took the water hoses and sprayed the workers. They continued to beat those who remained conscious. The fascists hit each person in the stomach with an iron bar until the poles went through their abdomens and reached the wall. The walls were covered in brains. Not one of the workers survived.

* * *

The fascist police confiscated merchandise from Jewish stores. For those Jews that departed and left their possessions behind, the police sealed off their homes and posted a sign that the home was now German property. On the 15th of July, 1941, a decree was proclaimed that every Jew, regardless of his gender or age, must wear a yellow star of David. It had to be ten centimeters by ten centimeters and sewn on the chest across the heart! Another law stated that Jews could not walk on the sidewalks but had to walk on the side of the road like geese. Other rules barred Jews from attending government institutions, forced them to give up their bicycles and radios, forbade telephone use, and traveling by train. Throughout the city, posters appeared with a familiar sign: "Jews forbidden!" The highest punishment, execution, was ordered for those that did comply with the laws. The area's commissioner, Ayortsion, signed the decree.

On the next day, an order appeared that all the Jews who lived in Kovno must transfer to an area in Slobodka. Nothing could be sold since everything a Jew owned was now German property. The Germans ordered that all the Jews from Kovno must move into Slobodka by the 15th of August 1941. Whoever remained outside the suburb's borders after that day would be shot. At the same time, the Germans ordered that a yellow patch had to be worn on the shoulder as well. The size of the symbol had to be the same size as the first one. In the Lithuanian newspaper, *I Lyseme*, horrible articles started to appear. All the poisons of German propaganda that had been published for years now penetrated into the Lithuanian newspapers where fascist agents and German-Lithuanian nationalists collaborated.

June 19, 1947: Bailly, Paris, France

Here is where my grandfather's first person account ends. The rest of his experience was gleaned from stories that he told orally and from historical records.

Behind the Fence

Even a mouse had more worth than a Jew.
- Rabbi Leib Schames

In the days prior to August 15th, 1941

Jews scrambled to find living quarters, but space was limited. Thirty thousand Jews had to relocate to an area that previously housed five thousand people.[47] Wealthier Jews exchanged their homes for a dining or an upstairs room. Some with contacts managed to receive a housing permit and find suitable quarters. It was harder for the poor to obtain housing. Despite all their efforts to find living quarters, many Jews were still left with nowhere to go. They stood in limbo, fearing reprisal but unwilling to live homeless in the ghetto.[48] On August 7th, 1941, Lithuanian fascists arrested those Jews who had not moved into Slobodka. They arrested people off the street, randomly taking any Jew who remained in the city to the Fourth Fort. After filling the quota, the Lithuanians transported the Jews into a small area near the fort and shot about one thousand Jews.[49] The mass execution shook everyone in the city. The Schames family, who lived a few blocks from the fourth Fort, quickly packed. Leib, his mother Chiene, and his four brothers and two sisters made their way across the bridge to Slobodka.

One could see thousands of Kovno Jews marching towards the Slobodka bridge with everything from clothes to kitchen wear. "All utensils cannot be taken except for electric ones," read the German decree, "two suits for men, four dresses for women, one chair per person, two plates each, one fork, a knife and a spoon each."[50] The order did not stop Chiene. She decided to smuggle in some of their valuables, including a gold necklace, other pieces of jewelry as well as three *sifrei Torahs*. The family lived a couple of houses down from the Panemune synagogue, and Chiene hid these scrolls with the rest of their possessions.[51] A family that rented the apartment complex behind them repossessed their home.[52] On Thursday, August 14th, every able-bodied Jewish man, heavily guarded by Lithuanian fascists, completed the ghetto fence. They lined barbed wire against seven foot high wooden poles, neatly erecting the metal lattice around the area.[53]

* * *

If one were only looking at the infrastructure – the dilapidated yeshivah building, the old horse market, the filthy, unpaved roads running crookedly through town – one would say that Slobodka looked as it always had. The lack of running water and the dark wooden houses. The suburb, an aura of raw immaterialism. The fence changed everything. Kovno Jewry lay on one side of the fence and the rest of Lithuania on the other. An atmosphere of isolation and loneliness pervaded Paneiru road, Democratu Plaza, and right over the fence, the Vilya River. The old suburb, once known for its traditional Jewish character, swayed with some thirty thousand lonely souls.

Ghetto residents could live in one of two areas, the Small Ghetto or the Big Ghetto. The Big Ghetto was located along the bank of the Vilya River. The Small Ghetto was located closer to the city. These two ghettos stood alongside one another. About 2,500 Jews lived in the Small Ghetto and 27,500 in the Big Ghetto.[54] The only way a Jewish resident could reach the Small Ghetto from the Big Ghetto and vice versa was to walk across an overhead bridge which ran across Paneiru street. Chiene and her seven children lived in the Big Ghetto.[55]

AUGUST 18TH, 1941

At the same time that the Jews were busy installing the fence, the German and Lithuanians ordered the Jewish council, the *Judenrat*, to recruit five hundred young men for work. "Work will be fair and take place indoors," the Germans explained, "there will be three meals a day."[56] Three meals a day was not something to be underestimated. Though many were hesitant, the news quickly spread around the ghetto and some voluntarily joined.

On the morning of August 18th, some four hundred doctors, engineers, and other professionals gathered at the ghetto gate. The Jewish ghetto police filled the quota and dragged people out of their homes. In all, five hundred and thirty-four people marched out of the ghetto towards city hall. The day passed. None of them returned. "They were held overnight to finish their work," the German authorities exclaimed. Families of the five hundred and thirty-four waited by the fence to find out what had happened to their loved ones. The Germans continued to assure them that the people will return soon. They were simply sent to work at the farms for the next few weeks.[57]

Rumors began to spread that Lithuanian fascists shot all five hundred and thirty-four Jews the day that they had left the ghetto. The *Judenrat* discovered that the reports were, in fact, accurate. Instead of taking the Jews to work, Lithuanian fascists lead the Jews to the Fourth Fort. They shot most of the Jews by a large pit near the fort and murdered those who managed to escape. Sturmfuehrer Fritz Jordan, German Commander of Ghetto

Affairs in Kovno, later explained that ghetto residents had stolen fifty packs of sugar. The Germans murdered ten Jews for each pack taken.[58]

The first ghetto roundup, or *Aktion*, was complete. Many young people in their twenties and thirties – the future leaders of Jewish-Kovno – had been killed. "In this very first *Aktion*," Leib explained, "they cut off the community's head."[59]

The end of August, the beginning of September

Kovno Jewry could not get any respite. The day after the *Aktion*, on August 19th, 1941, at around seven in the morning, German soldiers began conducting house searches, inspecting cellars, stalls, attics, and yards for valuables. They systematically surrounded a few blocks, barged into Jewish living quarters and confiscated wedding rings and suits as well as silver utensils and furniture. Leib decided to dig a hole in the ground and hide a gold necklace that his mother had smuggled into the ghetto. He would excavate the item after the inspection.[60]

After the first wave of searches, phase two began. On September 1st, the Germans grabbed six Jews and shot them in public. The following day, they took another six. They marched around the ghetto charging inhabitants with deliberately violating the law and then beat or shot the man of the house.

With the second phase complete, the Germans counted their spoils. It quickly became apparent that many items were still in Jewish hands. On August 18th, in the evening, Sturmfuehrer Jordan announced that house searches would continue until every Jew relinquished their commodities. The Jewish community would have two days to turn in their valuables. The Germans would shoot one hundred Jews if something was found after that time. Chiene was nervous. With the murder of her husband, she alone was responsible for her seven children. Keeping any possession of value was not worth the risk, and she forced Leib to hand over the necklace.[61]

* * *

The Jews tried to be as useful to the Germans as possible. Men, between fourteen and sixty, and women, between the ages of fifteen and fifty five, labored outside the ghetto at a German military airport at Alexot, known throughout the ghetto as the *Flugplatz*. They worked for some twelve to fifteen hours a day in various brigades in and outside the ghetto. The struggled each day at the worksite, laboring with pick axes and shovel, living with the illusion that the Germans would let them live if they continued with their duties.[62] The residents of the ghetto sincerely believed this. All outward signs seemed to signal that work meant life.[63]

On the evening of September 25th , 1941

The Germans informed the *Judenrat* that a Jew had fired a gun at a German guard. The *Judenrat* would have twenty-four hours to turn over the culprit. The entire episode was a fabrication, however. There was no perpetrator and no one to arrest. On Friday, September 26th, Germans, along with Lithuanian fascists, surrounded several blocks in the ghetto. They circled the area where the supposed crime had taken place. Residents were chased to the streets, beaten and driven into a nearby plaza. The Germans and their Lithuanian collaborators transported anyone with a work pass to one side. Those that did not own such pass, among them men, women, children and the elderly, were driven to the other. One could see hundreds of Jews marching to the Ninth Fort accompanied by armed Lithuanians. A long procession of people slowly walked up the streets leading towards the hill where the fort stood. The Lithuanians and their German counterparts murdered about a thousand Jews that night.

Those who remained, those with a work pass, were detained for several days. Lithuanian bandits burst into their homes and inspected each room. They searched through drawers and in cupboards. They broke walls, floors and examined closets, looking for stored valuables. Disregarding the occupants and looting the empty homes, the Lithuanians stole furniture and sacks of clothing.

The incarcerated Jews were allowed to move back to their living quarters after a few days. They had escaped the *Aktion* but suffered immediately. Every family who lived in the area lost a relative.[64]

* * *

There is a difference between the Lithuanian and the German. The Lithuanian spills blood and is attracted to it like a swarm of flies. He is ready to spill Jewish blood and lap up their possessions.[65] He kills savagely and in a disorganized fashion. He stands by the wayside, like a bear bereaved of food, eager to slay a Jewish mother and her child.[66] The Lithuanians are driven, almost by instinct, to murder Jews. The Germans, on the other hand, are more methodical. They attack slowly, first destroying the spirit and then the body. They outlaw communal prayer, forbid Torah study, and giving birth. They mistreat Jewish corpses, toss bodies into pits surrounding the Ninth Fort and in the Vilya River. They leave the community leaderless. The Germans attack the spirit and only afterward, do they attack the body.[67]

Yom Kippur October 1st, 1941

The Jews secretly gathered in the small room. Some Jews made a makeshift synagogue in the backyard next door to the Schames's living quarter. They used some of the *sifrei Torah* that Chiene had smuggled into the ghetto and poured out their hearts in prayer.

They asked G-d to save them from the upcoming trouble.[68] As the holiest point in the year commenced, sunset on Yom Kippur, all their fears came to mind. What had happened in the past few months? What had they experienced recently now that the Day of Reckoning was upon them? Their loved ones were taken away to the Seventh, the Sixth, the Fourth, and the Ninth Fort. Chased from their homes, into the ghetto, the Jews stood separate from the rest of the world. The past was bleak, and the future did not look promising.

For those living in the Small Ghetto, the next few days were filled with tension. Lithuanians around the Small Ghetto informed the Jews that they would soon have to vacate the area so they could move back into their old homes.[69] Other rumors spread that a large pit had been dug near the hospital in the Small Ghetto.[70] The residents of the Small Ghetto did not know where they would go. The Big Ghetto, as it was, was already full.

October 4th, 1941

It was late Shabbat night when it started. Fifty German soldiers along with about a hundred drunken Lithuanian fascists surrounded the fence at the Small Ghetto. A German stood in the middle of Paneiru Bridge stationed by a machine gun. Mobs of Lithuanian fascists and German officers piled into the Small Ghetto, driving every Jew, both the old and the weak, out of their home. They used their rifle butts to beat and chase the Jews into Sanjungos Square, Slobodka's old horse market.[71] As they had done in the previous *Aktion*, the Germans began sifting out the Jews who possessed a work pass. "Those with a pass," the guards exclaimed, "to the right." For those who did not possess a slip, "to the left." At times, the pass made little difference. Based on his cursory perception, a German officer sent the weak – mostly older men, women, and children – to the left, the strong – mostly the young – to the right. After several hours, Germans and Lithuanian fascists forced a hundred Jews from the left side to walk towards the gate at Paneiru Street. Heavily guarded, thousands of people made their way outside the fence.[72]

It was evident; Jews on the left side were heading toward the Ninth Fort. On both sides of Paneiru Street, Jews clenched to the fence and grievously looked at the scene, trying to take one last glimpse at their loved ones.[73] The Jews from the left side knew where they were heading. Many tried to escape on the way to the Fort. But, the Lithuanian fascists caught most of them, beat them with their rifle butts, and forced the escapees to continue on the march.[74] The Germans and Lithuanians shot some 1,500 Jews at the Ninth Fort.

Most tragic was the fate of the orphanage located in the Small Ghetto. The building housed around one hundred and eighty children whose parents had been murdered during the first month of the German occupation. The Jews realized that these orphans would be the first killed since they had little labor value. Despite their poverty, the community tried to feed and shelter these children. Indeed, for two months, they protected those that could not fend for themselves. Yet with swarms of armed Lithuanian and German guards surrounding the Small Ghetto, they could no longer help.[75] While German and Lithuanian fascists completed their work at the Ninth Fort, another group of Germans and Lithuanians gathered the orphans, teachers, and nurses, along with the elderly from the old age home onto trucks and hauled them to the Ninth Fort. Cries of anguish could be heard on both sides of Paneiru Street. Their efforts to protect the orphans had failed.

As Lithuanian partisans lead two thousand Jews to the Ninth Fort, another tragedy hit them.[76] Flames began to appear in the Small Ghetto hospital. Smoke could be seen over Paneiru Street. The Germans boarded up the doors to the hospital and forced two Jews to pour gasoline around the property. They nailed the doors and windows shut and set the building on fire. The patients, nurses, and a doctor remained inside. Sixty-two Jews – the head physician, Doctor Dawidowicz, two nurses, and the remaining patients – burned in the flames. The German and Lithuanian guards stood outside the hospital, making sure that no one inside escaped, and no one from the outside went in to help. As the flames burned, some of the patients tried to escape. They attempted to unlock the windows and attract the attention of the remaining Jews in the Small Ghetto. They yelled as loud as they could, piercing the hearts of the remaining survivors. The sound reverberated and repeated until finally, it fell silent.[77]

By evening, the German guards and the Lithuanian fascists finished. They chased the surviving Jews across the bridge into the Big Ghetto. Under a hail of blows and the erratic scream, about five hundred people rushed out of the Small Ghetto with some of their belongings.

The *Grosse Aktion*

Operation Barbarossa was in full swing. The German army marched eastward toward Moscow. Though they encountered resistance, *Wehrmacht* forces continued to capture territory. Between the months of July and August 1941, German soldiers crossed the Dnieper River, clearing the road to Smolensk and Moscow.

Despite inadequate resources and losses to their flanks, in the next few weeks Germany completed several land operations and air strikes. By mid-October, as they captured Moscow, German morale rose to an all time high. Soldiers wrote letters to their families that they would be home for Christmas. They told their children how they carried spoils from Russia.

* * *

During war, murder can be rationalized. Instead of earning respect for the kindness of one's deeds, in a time of war a person learns to be successful by the power of his sword. He is rewarded for violence. The more he kills, the more his peers admire him. The more he murders, the more he can survive. In a soldier's uniform, all laws of civility are lost. The brute and the barbarous are exalted while the weak are first to perish. After seeing the fields of battle, the soldier begins to justify his murderous acts. The evil inclination is ignited at the time of war.[78]

Some acts, though they are rooted in war, can never be rationalized. Some acts are so barbarous, so far from the realm of normalcy, that no one can explain their real cause. Someone might be able to justify that murder is natural in a time of war. But who can rationalize the *Aktions* of October 1941?[79]

* * *

With all the victories on the front, the mood in the ghetto became morbid. The Jews felt that no one would protect them. The Germans and their helpers would not be afraid to continue slaughtering innocent people.[80] These fears were warranted. Across the fence, rumors of another *Aktion* began to circulate in the ghetto. Local Lithuanians told ghetto inhabitants that Russian prisoners of war were digging large ditches around the Ninth Fort. Having recently suffered the loss of two thousand innocent people, anxiety increased. How many would they take? Whose turn was it this time?[81]

The rumors of another *Aktion* were slowly becoming a reality. On October 26th, 1941, Helmut Rauca, German commandant of Gestapo Security and Administrator of the Intelligentsia *Aktion*, told the Jewish Council that two ghettos would be formed: one for the employable and one for those who could not work. The Jews in the employable ghetto would receive higher rations. On October 27, the Germans handed out slips to those who worked at the *Flugplatz*. Like the Jordan pass, these papers indicated that residents were of working status. Finally, posters began to appear throughout the ghetto reminding the Jews to assemble at Democratu Plaza on October 28th for a census. Everyone had to arrive in the plaza by 6 a.m., even the young, the old and the sick.

The Gestapo would shoot anyone who stayed home.[82]

OCTOBER 28TH, 1941

Leib, his six siblings, and his mother Chiene began their march towards *Democratu Plaza*. They gathered in the square along with the rest of the ghetto, about 26,500 Jews in total.[83] At precisely 8 a.m., German policemen and Lithuanian fascists, with guns in their hands, entered the square.[84] Helmut Rauca followed. He stood on a large mound, mulling over the thousands of ghetto residents – men, women and children, the old, the young, and the sick. Rauca's face was filled with a sense of indifference about those whose fate he determined. His large eyes passed by each Jew, and with his thumb, he simply pointed to the right or the left.[85] Hitting with a barrage of blows, whips, and rifle butts, the Lithuanian guards drove the Jews to one side or the other depending on the officer's command.[86] Children were separated from parents, husbands from their wives, and families with small children were hauled over to the right.[87] Rauca sent Chiene, her five boys and two girls to the right.

Throughout the selection, the Jews were in a state of confusion. In the previous two *Aktions*, the left side meant death and the right side signified life. Now the "unproductive" – the old, the sick, and families with many children – stood on the right side. When Rauca realized that there were not enough people on one side, he began to send everyone in front of him to the right. All certificates were disregarded, even work passes. Rauca ordered men and women in their twenties and thirties to the right. A mixture of people – the strong and the weak – stood there while the Lithuanian police guarded the area. The Jews knew that one side meant life. "Which side was it?" was their only question.[88]

Chiene had an intuitive sense. Something did not sit well with her. She knew that the right side did not mean life this time. "Save yourself and slide to the left side," she told Leib. Immediately,

Leib encouraged his brother, Dov, to switch lines with him. "Let it be together!" he urged. But his brother wanted to stay with his mother and the rest of the family. As the minutes passed and the day came to a close, Leib heard his mother say, "Children, we are going, we will have the World to Come."[89]

Leib was hesitant. Maybe he could still convince his younger brother to come with him. His mother knew that Rauca would soon complete the selection. With her hands pressed against the center of his back, her brown eyes focused on saving her son, she pushed Leib. "One has to survive," she told him. With tears in his eyes, Leib ran to the left side.[90]

Throughout the day, Jews tried to move to the other side of the plaza. Some tried to escape to the right and some to the left; all of them believing that the side they were switching to meant life. The Lithuanian guards caught many of these Jews and drove them back to their respective line. "It was only by a *nes* [miracle] that I got through," Leib later explained.[91]

The ten thousand Jews who stood on the right side of the plaza, including Leib's mother, four brothers and two sisters, were brought to the Small Ghetto. The selection had lasted the entire day, and the Germans forced the Jews to spend the night in the abandoned area.

Early the next morning

Lithuanian fascists drove columns of one hundred Jews to the Ninth Fort.[92] Then they saw it – the Ninth Fort – a square fortification, the front partition, made up of red brick, standing some twenty feet high in the air. The back concrete structure attached to an elevated piece of earth. Told to wash up and undress, columns of Jews crammed into the Fort.[93]

The Germans and Lithuanian fascists drove one hundred people out of the barracks. They whacked anybody who did not move fast enough.[94] As the Jews ran outside, Lithuanian fascists, standing on an elevated plane, immediately pointed their machine guns and fired.[95] Most died from the gunshot. Yet by the time the next column came, some people from the previous group remained. They tried to escape. But surrounded by German and Lithuanian guards, there was nowhere to run. Except for a young boy, the Germans and their Lithuanian collaborators murdered every person who entered the Ninth Fort.[96]

* * *

A little less than half the ghetto had been wiped out. In one day, whole families were destroyed. Children and their parents, wives and their husbands, blood spilled without mercy, without reason or purpose. Filled with torment, they wept in desperation. Filled with mourning, they poured out bitter tears. Leib too cried. He too lamented:

> Can you imagine? Parents, they do so much and put in so much effort for their children and their grandchildren. This means everything to a Jewish family. Every human being cares about their children, but, I think, this is especially [true] of the Jewish people. The Lithuanians and the Germans brought them to a place, the Ninth Fort, and told them to undress. Then, they drove them into the pits. They drove them, you know, with sticks. They hit them with legs from a chair and smashed them if they did not move. And here, all the hope and perspective that you want to see from your children, all of it, they drove into the pit. Grandfathers, fathers, children, grandchildren, all of them; and they got shot. Do you know the cruelty?
>
> It is written in the Torah, "You should not slaughter a calf with its mother – *Oto V'Et Beno B'Yom Echad*".[97] Even for an animal, it is cruel to take a mother and her child to the

> slaughter. Here they took mothers and children together. It is a terrible, terrible thing. Can you imagine? What was my mother thinking? She was looking [after her children] – she had four boys and two girls. Right when we separated, she said, "*Kindelech Der get t'lu Olam Habah* – We are going, we will have the World to Come." But, you know, it was easier for them to get killed, but the pain of death was the same. It was easier for them to be killed because they believed that right away they would go and would have *Olam Habah*. But, they experienced the same pain as everyone else. Something more, when they shot the Jews, the bullet did not kill them right away. It could take many hours until the person died. It was terrible. But they went through it, there [in the Fort].[98]

Behind the fence, the survivors could only mourn. They saw what had happened. Germans and Lithuanians took ten thousand Jews from the right side and murdered them at the Ninth Fort. Older Jews in the Plaza died from exhaustion.[99] In total, Leib estimated that the Germans and Lithuanians murdered twelve thousand Jews that day, about one-third of the ghetto population.[100]

For many, the full force of the catastrophe did not sink in until weeks later. Slowly, the survivors began to realize which of their relatives and friends were missing.[101] For Leib, however, the full brunt of the *Aktion* sunk in immediately. In a twenty-four hour period he lost his mother, four brothers, and two sisters. He was a *yatom*, an orphan without any surviving relatives.

Feeling of regret filled his mind. Perhaps he could have saved his family. Maybe he could have pressed his brother to run with him to the left side. These feelings filled his mind throughout his time in the ghetto and for the rest of his life. "[If the selection occurred] now, I would have known what to do," he later said, "but, at the time, I just ran away from them."[102] Most of all, Leib and the rest of the ghetto wanted to take retribution. After the Great

Aktion, this *Grosse Aktion* as they called it, grave emotions began to fill their thoughts. "There was only one thing on our minds," Leib said, "we will take *nekamah* – revenge. But we couldn't, we didn't…we couldn't."[103]

The "Quiet Years"

With the latest *Aktion*, the Jews recognized they would not be able to escape death even if they worked. Too many young, healthy people had been killed.[104] Leib's mother was forty years old when she was murdered. Leib's siblings, his brother, Dov, and sister, Rochel, were only two years younger than him.[105] They certainly could have aided the Nazi war machine. However, the Germans were less concerned about supplying their armies. For them, exterminating the Jewish people was more important.

The survivors could barely continue their daily struggle. Why should a person perform arduous duties when a bullet would find him in a month? What was the purpose of delaying death and living the life of a slave laborer? Feelings of loss lingered in every house. The sense of "the same fate awaits you too" haunted each survivor. They were simply waiting for their end.[106]

The next day, October 29th, 1941, the Jewish work brigade did not leave for work. Apathetic to German threats, barely anyone showed up at the ghetto gate.[107]

Winter and spring, 1942

The Germans gave each Jew soup, referred to by the ghetto

as *yushnik*, made up of some horse meat, bones, and water. The soup lacked any nourishment. One could live off of the rations for a few weeks. But, depending solely on *yushnik* meant eventual starvation.[108] The ghetto population sunk into a depressed state. They reminisced about the *Grosse Aktion* and the travails that had taken place the past five months. Nevertheless, hunger soon began to take hold.[109]

Aside from *yushnik*, there were two ways to obtain produce. One could go outside the ghetto with their work brigade and trade for food with the Lithuanian population. Or, they could make a trade across the fence.[110]

Trading across the fence allowed residents to bring in large amounts of food. Lithuanian peasants lived near the ghetto and were willing to sell potatoes and flour. In a two-minute deal, a Jew could exchange a few dress shirts or a pair of pants for a whole bag of potatoes. However, Lithuanian and German guards walked along the ghetto fence, shooting anyone who stood close enough to the wire to make a transaction. Along the boundary of the ghetto, in German, Lithuanian, and Yiddish, a sign read: "Death Zone! Whoever approaches the fence will be shot without warning."[111]

A trader waited for the right moment to make a deal. She handed the Lithuanian guard a few dozen rubles and whispered, "Look the other way." Who knows, still? Who could trust the Lithuanian guards? The sentry might say that a deal could take place, but when the time came, he could shoot anyone who stepped within the two-meter death zone. A young woman's body lay on the ground, blood flowing from her forehead. Bartering across the fence would stop. But under the pressure of hunger, trading continued a few days later.[112]

Trading across the fence involved too much danger. Even if he could arrange a bribe, Leib did not trust the guards. He chose to trade miles away from the ghetto gate. In the morning, Leib smuggled out some merchandise with his work group. He took a piece of cloth with him. The next day some dress shirts. The following morning he wore two pairs of pants, first an old pair of pants from a Jew who had died in one of the previous *Aktions* and over this, his own pants.[113] When he reached the work site, he met with one of the gentiles whom he had spoken with the day before. Sometimes he just made a quick deal without any preparation, sneaking into an alleyway away from the worksite and arranging a trade with a Lithuanian peasant. He hid these goods in his trousers and smuggled the produce back through the ghetto gate.[114]

* * *

After coming back from labor one day, Leib met an old friend named Motke, who used to help Chiene and Yitzhak Meir in their flour and grain store. The two recounted the various *Aktionen* and noted the recent upturn in food coming into the ghetto. "I lead a band of girls and boys from the ages of twelve to sixteen," Motke reported. "This group of young smugglers have blue eyes and blonde hair. They look like Lithuanian gentiles and blend in well with the rest of the population." Motke gave each smuggler clothing, jewelry, and other items and sent them to spots where German surveillance was low. Knowledgeable about Kovno's layout and possessing a keen ability to arrange a trade, Motke stealthily administered transactions in various parts of the city. "Will you join?" Motke asked Leib, "my group is in need." "Yes," Leib responded without hesitation, "of course I will join."[115]

* * *

For six days a week, Leib worked at the *Flugplatz* and switched to another brigade in the city on Saturday. He made some trades at the airport, but it was inconsistent. Motke suggested that Leib join one of the city brigades. "I can get you into the roofer brigade in town," Motke explained, "there you will have more of an opportunity to trade. You will work at the *Flugplatz* only on Saturday."[116] As a trader on the ghetto's black market, Motke had connections with the labor office. In the next few days, Motke provided Leib with the necessary paperwork to change brigades. Leib did as he always had. At five in the morning, he took a pair of pants and lined up at the ghetto's entrance at Krisciukaicio Street. This time, however, he joined the roofer brigade.

* * *

A 100-kilogram pack of cement rested on his shoulders and back as he made his way up a few flights of stairs. He reached the roof, sweaty and exhausted. "Walk to the next side," the German master commanded. Leib walked along the two wooden planks which ran across each building. He carefully made his way, the wooden planks depressing under his feet, moving slowly from one roof to the other. The cement would eventually be used to flatten the roofs of wealthy Lithuanians.[117] It was a day mixed with harsh burdens and stealth trading. Leib worked with the roofer brigade from sunrise until sunset. At the half hour lunch break, he arranged new contacts and bartered with local peasants. Other times, he escaped during work hours. After carrying the heavy load, the sentries gave Leib an easier job. "Where's Schames?" the guards asked. "He's on the roof," another answered. Leib walked stealthily off site in search of contacts, the yellow badges neatly removed from his shirt.[118]

THE END OF AUGUST AND THE DAYS FOLLOWING

"Bringing food into the ghetto will be permitted only until August 26, 1942. After that, not even one gram will be allowed past the checkpoint. Additionally, after August 26th Jews will be forbidden to carry money."[119] On August 25th, a commotion erupted in front of the ghetto gate as people tried to search for a brigade that would give them a better opportunity to trade. People wrestled in front of the gate. They shoved and cursed at each other while the Jewish police and the Nazi Motorized Transport Corp demanded order.[120] The Germans whipped any ghetto resident who stepped out of his group, using their truncheons to hit those caught with a few rubles. Ghetto residents continued to push and shove, vying for a spot with a good brigade.[121] The atmosphere was tense all morning. German abuse continued until each brigade could be processed. Leib managed to keep his place with the roofer brigade. He took out his paperwork from his front pocket and showed it to the German officer. Finally, he marched out of the gate.

In the months following August 1942, the smugglers changed their strategies. No longer could they walk past the checkpoint without being searched. "You will need to bribe the Lithuanian guards today," the smugglers whispered, "when everyone comes back into the ghetto, you will give the guard a few rubles to let our brigade pass."[122] At night, when the commotion quieted, the smugglers gathered in their rooms to determine the best course of action. "We have little faith in the Lithuanians," they retorted, "We know we cannot trust them, but we need to. We should be able to carry contraband past the gate." When each act of smuggling meant risking one's life, the traders decided to hide larger packages under their shirt. Smuggling small parcels of food was just not worth the risk anymore.[123]

In late August and early September, smuggling became torturous for the young traders. They went through Krisciukaicio gate, each time with a new set of fears. The German commandant with his green overcoat stood by the checkpoint and confiscated smuggled goods. The guards whipped some of the younger Jews. They beat them with their truncheons.

Sometimes the brigades made a detour and entered the ghetto

through Varniu Street. The German commandant did not come by Varniu as often, and smugglers took advantage of this by carrying hundreds of packages of potatoes, matches, milk, pork, firewood, bread, flour, cigarettes, saccharines, butter and occasionally whiskey through the checkpoint. At first, the Lithuanian guards demanded a three hundred ruble bribe for each person they let through the gate. The smugglers agreed to the bribe. But after a few weeks, the cost rose. Some Jewish officers and labor office officials wanted to profit as well. They started acting as middlemen between the smugglers and the Lithuanian guards. "You must pay four hundred rubles for smuggling packages past the gate," the policeman demanded. A couple of days later, "Today you need to pay six hundred rubles!" A few days go by, "Eight hundred rubles!" It was heart-wrenching to pay so much. But the smugglers continued, bringing in hundreds of kilograms of produce past the checkpoint.[124]

* * *

To describe these scenes in words, ghetto inhabitants wrote songs to capture their fears.[125] Leib repeated one of these tunes:

At the ghetto gate,
A small fire blazes.
All around, great dread;
Jews now make their way
From the work brigades –
Each one in a sweat.
Should I walk on past,
Or should I stop, perhaps?
I do not know what to do!
The little commandant
In his green overcoat –
Wants what I want, too.

From the saucer, milk,
From the ladle, fat;
Jews, the heat is on!
A stick of wood,
Some money from the purse,
He grabs it from your hands!
Hey, comrade of the stripe,[126]
I'm not too "clean" tonight,
The checkpoint is drawing near!
Help me past the guard,
You'll get two pounds of lard,
And next day two more!
Stand in groups of four,
You stay with me here,
Don't you run ahead!
Tell that sentry there –
"All in order, sir!"
You'll have a loaf of bread.[127]

Leib appreciated these songs and would often recall how the ghetto faced their daily struggle bravely. "Jewish *koach* [power] is so great," he said, "even in a situation like this, we used to give others *chizuk* [strength]. We used to give ourselves *chizuk*."[128] Stiff necked and stubborn, ghetto residents continued their daily routine of work and trade. They adjusted to new conditions, adapted to ghetto living. Smuggling was not done for fame. Recognition never played a role in their minds. Under the threat of detainment at the ghetto detention center, flogging, being sent, along with one's family, to the Ninth Fort, and on most occasions, receiving a beating from a German and Lithuanian guard, matters of pride were of secondary importance. Surviving, living for the next day, selling the rest of one's goods to make a profit, this was their reward.[129] "I was either going to live or over – live," Leib recalled. He would either survive in health or exist with deprivation.[130] Regardless, he would live.

Leib gave all credit to Motke. Without him, he would have never been able to trade on a large scale. Without this friend who "stood right by him," as the tune goes, he would have surely starved.[131] It was not only Leib. Ralph Codikow, Leib's longtime friend and fellow survivor of the Kovno ghetto, explained how his mother used to ask a Jewish officer to beat her in front of the gate on her way back from work. The Jewish policeman yelled at Ralph's mom, screaming at her as she approached the ghetto. Ralph's mother appeared frightened, crying at the sight of the officer. In reality, though, the act was a ploy. The Lithuanian and German guards who monitored the gate believed that the Jewish policeman was merely doing his duty. The Jewish officer, however, was helping Ralph's mother, for after this "beating" the guard allowed Ralph's mother to carry a package under her girdle and into the ghetto.[132]

* * *

One evening, German and Lithuanian guards doubled at the gate. Three or four Germans, truncheons in hand, with five rifle-carrying Lithuanian policemen, ordered the Jews to line up in groups of four. One by one, the Germans and Lithuanian sentries came to each line and searched every Jew returning to the ghetto. Leib waited in the back of the line. He clutched a stick of butter close to his chest, his heart racing faster. The rumors of an inspection did not reach him. As the Lithuanian sentries ordered his brigade to line up, Leib threw the butter over the fence. The butter landed inside the ghetto, and two small children ran away with it.

One of the Lithuanian guards noticed him. The sentry ran over to Leib, cocked his rifle back and aimed at his forehead. For some reason, however, unbeknown to Leib, the Lithuanian guard lowered his weapon. As if the act of cocking his rifle itself was punishment enough, the guard allowed Leib to cross the checkpoint unscathed. Leib quickly made it past the checkpoint. He ran through the streets of the ghetto to search for the children who had taken his butter. He found them, gave them a piece and took the majority for himself.[133]

* * *

Motke was the group's leader, an outgoing administrator who increased each smuggler's chance at survival. With his knowledge of Kovno's layout and demographics, Motke directed his group and instructed them in trade. He was a well-known Panemune Jew. A gregarious orphan boy, he learned from an early age how to talk with people from different walks of life. As Motke walked down a ghetto street, he started conversations with brigade leaders and laborers. He introduced himself to leading workmen and menial professionals. Maybe someone could tell him what time a Lithuanian farmer came to trade? Perhaps, he could arrange a deal with the Jew himself? Who knew who would later prove helpful? *Judenrat* officials were not beyond his influence either. Using all these connections to his advantage, Motke became one of the principal leaders of the ghetto's black market.[134]

Residing with Motke was nothing like living at home. Motke's grandfather used to be a prominent religious leader in Panemune.[135] Motke participated in Ze'ev Jabotinsky's Zionist faction, *Beitar*, and believed in the group's ideas of Jewish autonomy and mass emigration to Palestine. He was confident and independent.[136] Jews came into his room at all hours of the night discussing Zionism and organizing trades for the upcoming days. The smugglers sat in a circle, dividing their loot and giving Motke his percentage. They sold some of the contraband on the street, making profits off the surplus.[137] These were Leib's new circumstances, a relatively fortunate existence, fastened upon him after the *Grosse Aktion*.

SEPTEMBER 1942

On Rosh Hashanah eve, the Labor office was compelled to assemble a group of one hundred and fifty Jews to dig peat in Palemonas. Located about seven kilometers from the ghetto, Palemonas was a swamp area situated along the Nemun River. Germans and Lithuanians forced Jews to dig for peat for long stretches of time. They were not afraid to use force to increase production or induce fear.[138] Labor office officials looked for young men without any family ties. Few would protest the transfer of a lone individual. Without any family, administrators at the Labor Office placed Leib's name on the list.[139]

In the middle of the night, the Jewish ghetto police came to Motke's living quarters and climbed the attic steps. "Get up!" a police officer exclaimed. Leib woke up startled. Three men stood above him. "Get up!" the policeman said again as if the first warning was not enough. Two of the officers grabbed Leib by his legs, the other by his neck. The policemen dragged him outside toward the ghetto's detention center.[140]

Leib stood in a tight wooden room. He could make out a few faces as he waited behind the iron prison bars.[141] The doors opened and closed a few more times as other Jews joined him. Men and women walked past the jail looking at the new inmates waiting to be transferred.[142] Leib would die at Palemonas. With new prisoners entering the cell every few hours, the reality of this became all the more palpable. Outside his cell, Leib saw some children playing. On a small piece of paper, he wrote a note, "Get Motke." He threw the paper through the cell bars. The children understood. They scoured the ghetto in search of Motke. Probably because, like Motke, many of the Jewish ghetto police belonged to *Beitar*, Motke managed to procure Leib's release and remove his name from the list.[143]

* * *

A few weeks later, Leib smuggled a large piece of smoked ham into the ghetto. He put it into the smuggler's pile and hoped to allocate his provisions the next morning. However, when he woke up, the ham was gone. "What happened?" Leib asked Motke. Motke explained that he had lost it.[144] Leib was upset. He had risked his life to obtain some food, and now Motke lost it. Yet, Leib kept his mouth shut. He owed Motke his life. Remembering what had happened in the cell a few weeks earlier, he could never complain. "Motke saved my life," he recalled, "I could not say a word."[145]

* * *

The Nazi Motorized Transport Corp supervised Jews throughout the ghetto. They marched back and forth within the ghetto fence, reprimanding, casting fear, and beating those who did not comply with orders. No longer were they stationed outside the ghetto as in months past. Instead, they stood inside the ghetto fence monitoring the people when they walked between their homes, making sure that each of the Jews displayed their yellow star and removed their hat as they entered and exited the gate.[146] No longer could a Jew just switch brigades at the gate.

At five a.m. on Saturday, Jewish police officers walked from house to house, pounding on the wooden shutters. "Rise for work at the airport," the policemen announced. The laborers quickly dressed and ran towards the gate. Barely awake, they lined up one in front of the other, four to a row, until twenty-five rows were counted. "One hundred people," the Jewish officer announced. The column of one hundred Jews marched past the gate. As each column exited the ghetto, Lithuanian officers abused the workers, throwing jibes, mocking and beating those who veered from their place. Thousands of Jews marched sixteen kilometers to the *Flugplatz*, from Slobodka to Alexot.

Leib worked on the huge expanse. He grabbed a pick with his hands, methodically hitting the dirt under his feet and removing any protruding rocks. Along with the rest of laborers, Leib loaded the gravel onto wheelbarrows, clearing one area, tipping the wheelbarrow, and then flattening the ground. He dumped dirt into cement mixers, carrying bags of sand and wooden beams around the worksite. At random, the German guards degraded the workers, beating anyone who stepped out of line or did not work fast enough. Thousands of Jews dug ditches, lined drains, completed cement work, and labored from dawn until dusk, some twelve to fifteen hours straight to construct a runway.[147] Maybe Leib could have traded at the worksite secretly or on the way back from the airport. But it was never consistent. Leib moved back and forth, working Saturday at the *Flugplatz* and the other six days with the roofer brigade, trying to arrange a deal whenever possible.[148] Leib repeated a ghetto tune to describe working at the Flugplatz:

I will sing, friends,
A song that weeps from the heart.
I will tell you where I live; I will tell you everything about it.
In the morning, when the sun rises, it is still dark.
My bones are aching from the day before.
Your clothes are torn, they are hanging, wet.
The boots are still soaked from yesterday.
Small children are carrying gravel.
They don't have anymore strength.
The German is whipping them.
He is shouting a few curses and bad spirits.
The food that he gave, whatever food it was, is water and cabbage.
You have to look for it.
Maybe you will find a little bit of cabbage, but you

have to scrape the edge of the pot to find it.
Do not lose your hope or belief.
Not forever is trouble.
Not forever is slavery.
Not forever is suffering.[149]

Leib worked from dawn until dusk, and then again from dawn until dusk. The days and nights seemed to mesh together, only to be interrupted by shouting guards and the master's eyes filled with enmity. When Leib returned to Motke's attic, the next day of hard labor was soon around the corner.[150]

Winter – Summer, 1943

Arrests started to increase. In a three-day period in the beginning of February, the Germans and their Lithuanian collaborators caught a man walking away from his brigade, a Jewish family trying to make a deal, and a band of smugglers in the midst of a trade. A Lithuanian officer brought a group of women to the Lithuanian police station.[151] The next day, Lithuanian and German guards arrested twenty-six Jews – some young men but mostly elderly Jews, women, and a handful of children. They sat behind the precinct's iron bars, imprisoned for trading. The Gestapo entered the detention center and transported the twenty-six Jews to the Ninth Fort for breaking the rules and regulations of the ghetto.[152] Sorrow filled the streets. The smugglers, especially, felt the brunt of the latest roundup. They feared for their lives. The latest *Aktion* confirmed their worst fears: smuggling will be punished with death.[153] Yet despite the harsh edict, the smugglers continued to trade and transport across the gate. They continued to take chances that most ghetto residents were simply unwilling to take.[154]

The Jews of the ghetto continued with their everyday routine. They tried to make sense of their world, bearing their suffering, normalizing the past, and remaining determined for the future.[155] They still hung on to the most minute hope. "Perhaps we will survive?" they thought, "Maybe we will only need to work? There is still a chance for us to live with our Lithuanian neighbors."

For Jews like Leib, making it through the day was their main activity. Though Kovno Jews formed an orchestra, sponsored cultural activities, gathered for Torah study, and created underground Zionist groups, for him, scrounging for his next meal became his prime concern. Escaping the harsh weather conditions and finding firewood, especially during the winter months of 1941 and 1942, became a reality. The months slowly passed by, and winter 1943 was coming to an end. Sixteen thousand Jews remained.[156]

* * *

Slowly, residents became aware that the ghetto, which was run previously by the Gestapo, would be transferred under the auspices of the S.S. The residents knew about the S.S. and how they liquidated other ghettos. In the eyes of the ghetto population, the S.S. was different from the Gestapo in that they were more experienced at committing mass murder.[157] With the liquidation of the Warsaw ghetto and the recent massacres at Ponar, the news of the S.S. arrival became all the more demoralizing. On September 15th, 1943, the S.S. commandant, Wilhelm Goecke, became governor of the Kovno ghetto.[158]

Before Goecke arrived, the S.S. commander was known throughout the ghetto as an expert at murder.[159] It was common knowledge that he had been a commandant in several concentration camps throughout Germany. Yet, as soon as he arrived, Goecke began to institute small, almost tolerant reforms. He increased the ghetto's food rations and relaxed checkpoint security. Goecke spent his first days in Kovno walking up and down the streets of Slobodka, obtaining information about the

Jewish population, their work dynamics, and the area's layout.[160] To the inexperienced eye, it seemed harmless. After a few weeks, however, the commandant revealed his true self. Goecke started shutting down certain brigades and concentrating workers in smaller units. Each brigade would be closely monitored by the S.S. Jews would have little contact with Lithuanians.[161] Finally, Goecke raised the gauntlet. Out of the all the bad news that had come with his arrival, Goecke had one more suprise.[162]

October 8, 1943. Yom Kippur

Many Jews gathered for prayer in a cleared out hospital. Packed, with barely enough room to stand, a ghetto Jew raised his voice:

> Men and women of the ghetto. What have we witnessed? What has happened to our loved ones, our wives and husbands, our children and friends, these last two and a half years? We have seen their blood spilled. We have seen them driven into pits. (Murder without reason or purpose!) Never before has a people been driven to such insanity. Never before has the murder of innocent women and children been lauded. Never before has the beating of an elderly man been rewarded by the government and the shooting of thousands of innocent people been encouraged. The massacres committed these last two and a half years overshadows thousands of years of criminal history.
>
> Yet, history will not care what happens to us Jews. The world has never cared about our misfortune. They will certainly overlook our current state. Do not rely on the nations of the world. Even with all their victories on the front, the Allies will not come to our aid. They have already shown that they will not help us in our time of need. I therefore admonish you: save yourself. Run to the partisans. Go into hiding. I want you all to know that this will be the last Yom

> Kippur in the ghetto. At this time next year, there will be no ghetto. And yet despite it all, we must survive. We must live so that the world – a world which has deliberately tried to forget our misfortune – will know what has happened here. *Le Shana Tova Tekhatemu* – I wish you all a year of life.[163]

The sentence, "this will be the last Yom Kippur in the ghetto," scared the audience.[164] With all the changes in the ghetto, the Jews understood it to be true. Leib heard the speech. He knew, as well, that the ghetto was to be liquidated.[165] The entire ghetto, the old wooden houses which lined Slobodka's streets, would be demolished. Motke would be gone. His attic, where he prepared for the upcoming day, would also be gone. It was bound to happen; the Germans were going to convert the ghetto into a concentration camp.[166]

Simchat Torah, October 22, 1943

On this day, the men and women of the ghetto were completely in their element. They felt in their own frame of mind.[167] The men wrapped their hands together and sang, "*Ana Hashem, Hoshe'ah Na* – Please G-d save us, please Master save us on the day we call to You."[168] The people in the background began to clap their hands in order to join with the rest of the congregation. They sighed in chorus with all the Jews. The deep-seated melancholy that once pervaded the room now evaporated. In its place, a feeling of joy spread. There is a story about the Gaon of Vilna, the Torah genius known throughout Lithuania, who danced with great exuberance on *Simchat Torah*. Normally, the Gaon involved himself with matters of Torah. He spent the majority of his days reviewing the Babylonian and Jerusalem Talmud and occupied himself with books of Kabbalah. He slept for half hour intervals in order to continue his studies at night. On this *Simchat Torah*, however, his seriousness disappeared. As the ark opened and the leaders took out the scrolls, the Gaon enthusiastically danced with the rest of congregation. He rejoiced, sang, and joyously grasped the Torah, celebrating with the entire community. As the sun set and that great day ended, the Gaon of Vilna came back to his normal routine. His elation dissipated. He opened his books and returned to the reality of the everyday, to the study of Torah.[169] For these Jews, the day was filled with a mixture of somberness and joy. Leib walked around the room, lifting the *sefer Torah* above his head with great passion. Happiness filled his heart. But as soon as the dancing ended, reality – the reality of the ghetto – returned.[170]

The Kovno Concentration Camp

Yesterday is gone, one's family is gone, one's honor is gone, one's house is gone. Nothing is left, except You, Master of the Universe, and I.[171]

- Rabbi Mordechai Pagramanski, ghetto resident

In mid-October, Goecke forced the *Judenrat* to prepare three thousand names. The people on the list would be transferred thirty miles away from Kovno to a little village along the Neman River called Ezerelis. The *Judenrat* posted a list of three thousand Jews.

October 25-26, 1943

The men, women and children on the list decided that living in hiding was better than deportation. No one trusted the Germans. Jewish families hid behind walls. Children took cover in drawers and closets.

In the morning, the Jewish ghetto police, along with the Germans, searched the ghetto to find those people on the *Judenrat's* list. They scoured the ghetto. Hundreds of Lithuanians and Ukrainian men followed.[172] The Lithuanians and Ukrainians surrounded several buildings in the ghetto with their rifles and truncheons. They broke doors and windows, destroying furniture and walls. Bloody, some unable to stand upright, residents fled to the street. After a few minutes, the Lithuanians and Ukrainians chased the Jews to the ghetto's gate and towards trucks located outside the ghetto.

Upon reaching the quota, the Germans drove the trucks to the train station near the *Flugplatz*. "Children to one side of the platform," the guards demanded, "men and women to the other. The men and women in separate cattle cars, the children on the other train." Overwhelmed by the mass of people, the Jews stood in the cattle cars, pressed against one another. The Germans sent the men and women to Estonia, Vavaria, and Klooga to build fortifications for the German army. They transported the children to Auschwitz.[173]

* * *

It is dark at night, veiled in mourning.
The sky is black, stars do not shine (all of nature is mourning).
The ghetto is surrounded in darkness.
The Jews look around with terror and pain,
They looked up our names.
And it makes no difference what we think.
No difference our thoughts, party or goals.
Everyone with yellow patch is shot, there is no distinction.
The symbol of the ghetto is the feeling of the diaspora.
They searched and drove us from our houses.
They forced us to leave behind everything we had (wealth and possessions).
Lonesome, we survived.

Nobody to comfort us, without help or protection.
Strange nations (Lithuanians and Ukrainians), they antagonize.
They spread like fire for pogroms and murder.
Every day, they take us from one place to another; to extermination (*Aktions*).
They took us to the graveyard of the Ninth Fort.
They took off their clothes and threw them into the pit alive.
Nazi machines and armaments fire; guns blaze like a fire.
In that fashion they murdered.
A mother ran to the German sergeant and begged to spare the life of her child.
He laughed it off, a shot was his answer.
The mother fell and next to her the child.
The troubles are terrible and the pain is even greater – for death runs after you.
Everyone lost a piece of their heart – there in the Ninth Fort.
Mother, child, sister and relative.
Mothers do not cry anymore, they should not cry anymore for brothers.
The deep wounds and a bloody heart.
Heal yourself with the hope, for out of the graves we will take revenge.[174]

In the beginning of November, 1943

Sixty-four Jews, made up mostly of arrested ghetto escapees and smugglers, were forced by the Gestapo to open the pits and incinerate the bodies near the Ninth Fort. The bodies were not only Kovno Jews. Including some twenty-five thousand Kovno Jews, an estimated ten thousand Jews deported from Germany, Austria, and Czechoslovakia, as well several hundred Soviet prisoners of war, were also buried in the pits surrounding the Fort. No one missed the smoke which rose to the sky. For the surrounding population, hell itself was burning. For the Jews, our brothers and sisters were burning, our own flesh and blood was turning to ash.[175]

In November 1943, the S.S. began transforming the ghetto into the Kovno Concentration Camp. The Germans started evacuating a few blocks in the ghetto known to them as Block B.[176] Everyone in the area, families that felt the brunt of the latest *Aktion*, had to evacuate within forty-eight hours and find a new apartment. Congestion rose to an all-time high as units that once housed three or four people now contained eight to ten.[177]

A few days later, Goecke started to split the ghetto up according to work groups. The small brigades were combined into larger groups that would work in eight labor camps outside Slobodka. Each group would live in barracks near the worksite. First, the Germans established a camp at the *Flugplatz* in the suburb of Alexot. Next, they organized camps in Sanciai, another Kovno suburb, where one thousand and two hundred Jews would sleep and work.[178]

Before the camps could be established, the Germans needed to create barracks, manage guards and build a surrounding fence. This took some time and for the first few weeks, the Kovno Concentration Camp was there in name only.[179] Goecke, though, continued expanding restrictions. Surveillance over the work brigades increased. Additional policemen escorted each brigade. Only large groups of people were allowed to travel to the worksite, and then only through alleyways and small streets.[180] Motke's group would need to be more conscious of the guards and locate Lithuanian traders with precision and covertness.

By late November, the Germans completed the camps. One thousand Jews were moved to Alexot, followed two weeks later by another nine hundred Jews to Sanciai, followed by Palemonas, Keidan, and Koshedar. The Germans organized each camp according to the type of production. One camp was devoted to aviation. Another to peat, bricks, and rubber.[181] With thousands of Jews residing in the satellite camps, the ghetto was left desolate. Some two thousand people remained in the workshops, including the *Judenrat*, the Jewish police, some smaller brigades, as well as the old and the sick. Within the ghetto, Goecke expanded the ghetto workshops, increasing production and labor efficiency.[182] Leib worked with the smaller brigades in the ghetto and managed a few deals.[183]

FEBRUARY, 1944

Leib tried to avoid the deportations to the satellite camps. But by late February, the *Judenrat* forced Leib, Motke and about five hundred others to work in Alexot at the *Flugplatz*

After a few hours in Alexot, Leib saw how different the camp was from the ghetto. Everyone slept on two-tier bunks. The prisoners lived in wooden buildings called blocks. The Germans carried out a roll call every morning, and the sexes were separated. When the prisoners woke up, they did not march outside the fence as they used to but slept at the worksite. Aryan Capos whipped a inmate who worked slowly. They sometimes transported the entire block to the Ninth Fort if a prisoner was found missing.

* * *

Despite these radical changes, Motke was not fazed. He adapted to his situation, facing each of his troubles with determined vigor and a stubborn sense of pride. With his help, Leib managed to find some trading opportunities in the camp. Motke walked along the camp barracks with a pair of scissors and cut holes at the bottom of the fence. He instructed his group, children under the age of eighteen, to form groups of two and slip through the hole to trade and pump water from a nearby well.[184] "If you will not do it," Motke explained to the children, "you will die."[185]

One person in Motke's group, Judith Meisel, a fifteen-year-old smuggler, injured herself while crawling through the camp fence. She came back to Alexot, her back lacerated. "I had always lied to my mother and said that I obtained food from charity," she reported. With the deep bruises on her back now, she could no longer hide the truth. Her mother prohibited her from assisting Motke again.[186]

Piece by piece, Motke cut holes throughout the fence and administered trades. The Jewish police, having realized that someone was destroying German property, scoured the camp in search of the perpetrator. They never found Motke. Among the Jewish masses, behind the barracks and the fence, Motke continued to operate his group. He traded and smuggled despite the harsh decrees and enclosure that surrounded them.[187]

The Kinder Aktion

March 26, 1944

Worries and pessimistic fears reached new heights. Rumors of another *Aktion* began to spread through the ghetto. On March 26, Goecke ordered the chief of the Jewish police, Moshe Levine, to report to his quarters to prepare for an air-raid inspection. The Jewish police marched into Demokrotu Plaza at 8 a.m. They stopped in front of S.S. headquarters. With several German officers beside him, Goecke inspected the officers. He separated some from the line and told the rest to sit on the ground. As the selection took place, dozens of trucks, all painted white, surrounded the ghetto. A few parked near the Jewish police.[188]

Minutes later, the Germans began driving the white trucks throughout the ghetto. With loudspeakers attached to the vehicles. they ordered: "Everybody must stay in their home or else you will be shot."[189] As the Germans drove through the street, they blared jazz music through the car's loudspeakers. Those nearby quickly sprinted home. Others ran into random rooms or towards the nearest alleyway. The streets were clear in a few minutes.[190] After the Germans finished with the streets, Ukrainians rushed into the ghetto on foot in search of Jewish children.[191]

Jews gave their children sedatives and shoved them into drawers.[192] They placed them under bundles of clothing, in barrels, and beneath linens. Mothers held their children tight. Before placing their children in hiding, they quietly sobbed, "Do not come out of your place or onto the roads, the enemy is everywhere."[193] The Ukrainian and Germans found many of these places. Between the light murmurs and the disturbed dressers, it was not hard to tell. The mothers screamed. The Germans yelled, "There is no need for a Jew to have children!"[194] The Germans and the Ukrainians dragged many of the children toward Varniu Street and threw them into the white trucks parked in front of the S.S. building.[195] Some of the mothers jumped into the vehicles along with their children. "Wherever you will go I will go," they said, "Wherever you will die, I will die, and there I will be buried."[196]

Ukrainian bandits also took Jews who were too sick to work and the elderly. They surrounded the ghetto hospital and forced patients to march towards the trucks. Passes were ignored; so were their pleas. Eventually, the Germans deported some one thousand people to Majdanek and Auschwitz.[197]

As this was going on, Goecke and the Gestapo kidnapped the Jewish police, all those who had lined up in front of the S.S. building, and transported them to the Ninth Fort. The Germans interrogated one hundred and fifty Jewish policemen about the partisans and the whereabouts of ghetto hideouts. "Where are the bunkers?" they demanded.[198]

Many Jewish officers refused to disclose this information and were murdered as a result. Some of the policemen, however, cooperated and revealed the location of the bunkers.[199]

March 28, 1944

The Ukrainians and Germans continued the searches. This time, they came with bloodhounds, axes, picks, and grenades, marching orderly throughout the ghetto, smashing walls and furniture. The Germans deported to Auschwitz and Majdanek some eight hundred children, older adults and the unemployable.[200]

On March 27th and 28th, the same type of *Aktion* took place in Kovno's satellite camps – Shantz, Koshedar, Keidan, and Leib's camp, Alexot.[201] The *Aktion* was so thorough in some camps that not one child escaped deportation. Prisoners from Alexot left for work on March 27th and, as always, children and the elderly remained behind in the barracks. When Leib and the rest of the laborers returned from the *Flugplatz,* they realized that the children had been taken to the train station.[202]

Parents ran around the camp crying hysterically. They screamed at the top of their lungs searching mindlessly for their children. Perhaps there was a slight possibility that their children escaped deportation. When nightfall came, the shock of losing their children dissipated. But the sobs continued.[203] The *Kinder Aktion* was over; more than two thousand people were taken.[204]

* * *

Grasp life by the seconds, despite the knowledge of your end. We can survive one more day, we can take another breath of life.[205] Scrapping for existence, trying to escape the cruel and the vicious. Can you imagine Kovno Jews at this time? Can you see their faces and their children, no longer there or secretly hidden?

The ghetto was to be liquidated, the work brigades and the *Judenrat* disbanded. Jews went into the same hiding places that they had used during the *Kinder Aktion.* Some took their chances with Lithuanian contacts while others escaped to the partisans. About fourteen thousand Jews remained in the old ghetto and the surrounding camps.[206]

ON JULY 8, 1944

Liquidation began. Germans, Lithuanians, and Ukrainians searched through the ghetto and deported everyone that they found. The Germans murdered some surviving children and then proceeded to burn down ghetto hospitals, lumberyards, barns, workshops, and homes. Many who remained in hiding perished in the flames. Over the years, the Germans had reduced the ghetto's size some ten times. This act, however, represented the ghetto's final blow, the end of a Jewish community which had resided in Kovno for over five hundred years. The Germans and their helpers murdered about two thousand Jews during the liquidation of the ghetto.

Stutthof

The Russians moved westward. Those still alive, hiding in bunkers, heard bombs exploding nearby. Stuck between liberation and deportation, the Jews waited in silence. A handful of survivors who hid in select spots throughout the old ghetto managed to survive when the Russians entered Lithuania a few days later.

The Germans transferred Leib to the satellite camp at Keidan, a few miles away from Slobodka. A few weeks later, the Germans deported him again.[207] Black fog stretched across the sky. The sounds of gunshots and the smell of smoke permeated the air. As the Russians slowly made their way into Kovno, the prisoners marched to the *Flugplatz*.[208]

Forty cattle wagons lined the train. Each wagon had a tiny barred window on top and some straw on the floor. Fifty Jews lay in their own filth. Piled onto the train, hands and feet, shoulders and arms, they sat there pressed together like cheap merchandise. "That's fifty," announced the guard, "everyone else to the next cart."[209]

Despite the nauseating air, the inmates tried to fall asleep. They all stood cramped against one another, some of them mindlessly dazed, others, with their shirts over their mouth, attempting to fall asleep. A man urinated in the corner of the wagon. Another passed out from the lack of oxygen. After a few hours, the doors of the wagons opened. "Everyone out," the guard shouted, "relieve yourself across the field." The Germans kept guard while the men ran towards the grassy area a few feet away and urinated. The women followed. A half an hour passed until the Germans ordered everyone back to the train.[210]

After a few hours in the cattle cars, the train stopped at a second platform. The Germans gave the Jews a watery soup and ordered them to run to a second cattle car on the other side of the platform. This train was no different from the first – the same air, the same space, and the same foul smells. Another fifty people entered each cart.[211]

The train traveled for a few minutes, passing little homes, some small cottages and a quaint forest. Women worked in their gardens. Children played in the front yards. Out of the picturesque forest, however, the train made a sharp turn. Suddenly a barbwire fence stood in focus. The wire wrapped along the wooden planks. It ran upward and horizontally, curving circularly along its rim. The contrast between the beautiful village and the fence seemed to shock the prisoners. Beyond the fence, a high chimney replaced the German women. Wooden bunkers replaced the trees. Prisoners in black and white garb replaced the small houses.[212]

July 25th, 1944

After an arduous two and a half day journey, the train came to a stop.[213] Large S.S. soldiers, with rifles in their hands, dressed all in black with a skull insignia on their helmets, rammed the doors open. "Get out," they ordered, "line up." The Jews assembled in a column of five. They quickly saw, written in big letters on the gate – Stutthof.[214]

Leib and his group marched to a large warehouse, visible to everyone on the other side of the camp. Eyeglasses, artificial limbs, dolls, toys, human hair and thousands of shoes lay along the wall of the warehouse. The objects lay there in a pile, like a giant anthill. "All men, stand up," an S.S. guard ordered, "and line up at the warehouse exit."[215]

The men marched out of the warehouse towards the plaza. After waiting for a few minutes, an S.S. guard approached the group. "You will be brought to the showers," he explained, "nothing can be brought in with you. Undress and leave all your valuables here; we will return in fifteen minutes."[216] Not knowing whether this was an *Aktion* or another prerequisite before entering the camp, the inmates removed everything: watches, coins as well as all their clothing.[217] Fifteen minutes later, the German came back and ordered the group to line up. German guards, along with several Polish prisoners of war, Capos with whips in their hands, ordered the naked prisoners to form a column. The guards grabbed the prisoners, throwing each one on the table to search for valuables. The Capos forced Leib onto the table and performed a rectal exam to see if he was hiding anything. The Capos then shaved off the hair on his head and the rest of his body.[218]

After the examination, Leib was given a small, sandy bar of soap and ordered to run to the next room. Showerheads filled the entire room and water trickled from the pipes. A few seconds later, the guards ordered the prisoners to move to the next room. Leib picked up a striped hat, a black and white shirt and a pair of pants. On the floor lay the most vital item of all: a pair of wooden shoes.[219]

Nothing came through the showers of Stutthof.[220] All personal mementos and religious items were left outside. A Jew could not even carry a shirt through the showers, let alone a pair of *tefillin* or a prayer book. Could Jews blow the *shofar* in the camps?

"Something like this," Leib said, "could never happen."[221] Maybe a Jew could pray, but that was only if they knew the prayers by heart. The ghetto was far. Practice faded away. A prisoner's mentality set in.[222]

On July 26, 1944

The Germans brought Leib and the rest of his barrack to a large storage unit where they were told to undress. The group stood naked in the cold. Leib was forced to return the prisoner's garb and find other clothes. He looked in a pile for a good pair of pants and a decent shirt. He found some wooden clogs, a torn pair of pants and a shirt infested with lice.[223]

A German S.S. guard came to the group and reported that the group would be evacuating Stutthof. They would only spend one night in the camp. Leib walked back to the train station.[224] Crowded with another forty-nine men, the wheels screeched as the train moved along the steel rails.[225]

* * *

There is a story about the Vilna Gaon who, while arguing with his brother over a piece of Talmud, began to laugh at his brother's interpretation. The Gaon's brother said to him: "You are such a *tzaddik* and yet you make fun over your own brother." The Gaon then took out a little kerchief from his pocket and waved it. His brother then noticed their mother standing there, rejoicing in her children learning Torah – *em ha'banim semecha* – a glad mother of children. The Gaon then explained to his brother that he did not laugh at him, G-d forbid, but was smiling at their mother who had just come into the room.

Dear Jewish brothers, if only I could be a Gaon of Vilna and wave a little kerchief so you could see the true reality of things. You would be able to see our fathers, mothers, brothers, and sisters, our children and our wives as they were murdered. What kind of horrible, torturous, *anuyim kashim* [harsh afflictions] did our loved ones go through until they finally left this world? How they suffocated in the gas chambers. They were rounded up in the chamber and then gas was released. These people died so horrifically! As the gas came into the room, people gagged and blood started to flow through every cavity of the body. Because of their affliction, people grabbed each other by the hair. An hour later, after this horrible act was performed, the bodies laid there, stuck and interlocked to one another. Picks had to be used to tear them apart. The goal was to commit this tragic and barbaric act yet leave the area entirely bloodless. They laid them down on planks and transported them to the crematorium. They carried up to two hundred people on each cart. In a twenty-minute period, people who recently had the strength to live and possessed the hope for a better tomorrow completely disappeared. There was no sign left of these people.

Here, in the crematorium, everything ended. Whole transports arrived with young children. With the train cars sealed, they traveled an entire week, from their designated area to the crematorium, without a bite of food or a drink of water. When the transports arrived, the car doors opened, and everyone inside was found dead. They died from the hunger and the cold. They then were burned. Some transports would come with husbands and wives with their children. The stronger men were allowed into the camp to work, but women and their children were sent to the crematorium.

Imagine the picture; a husband is separated from his wife forever. The bandits then tear a child away from a mother's arms and hit the child over the head with an iron rod. The mother witnesses all that is done to her child; afterward, the child is burned. And after, the mother is taken to the gas chamber and burned in the crematorium. Two months later, the husband is brought. He looks like the living dead, all skin and bones. Tortured from hunger and the deadly strikes, he lacks the energy to bear the strenuous workload. Everything is burned in the crematorium. Everything goes out with the smoke that rises from the big chimneys. "And the Children of Israel should cry over the fire which Hashem burnt."[226]

* * *

The prisoners sat in the cattle cars starving, their eyes sunken. They ate some beet soup apportioned at the stops. The inmates rested on the wooden ground, huddled and pressed against one another. Corpses lay in the cattle cars, resting, motionless, on the floor. It was a seventy-two hour ride when the train stopped at "Kaufering." The two-day journey to Stutthof and then the three-day journey to Kaufering left Leib disoriented. He tried to put together the details as quickly as he could. He was at a train station called Kaufering. He was close to the city of Landsberg. "Everyone out," the guard yelled. Leib and the rest of the group jumped out of the train.[227]

Tisha B'Av, July 29th, 1944[228]

The S.S. kicked the prisoners, struck them with their batons and ordered them to form a line in columns of one hundred. The prisoners marched for a few miles towards Landsberg, making their way past a dusty road towards Kaufering I, one of the eleven subcamps under the jurisdiction of Dachau.[229] The guards counted the prisoners. They issued a few items: a towel, a blanket, a bowl, and a spoon. They gave them some soup, made up of mostly water and a few vegetables, and ordered the prisoners to move into the barracks. The new inmates collapsed on the straw that lined the barrack walls.[230]

MOLL

A whistle was the first thing that they heard. The morning wake-up call created a frenzy among the inmates. Like a stampede, the prisoners pushed and shoved to the *Appellplatz* at 5 a.m. Two thousand prisoners assembled in the yard.[231]

In groups of a hundred, the inmates marched outside the camp. They walked four miles past the forests and a small town. Below the trees and greenery, declining downwards, the prisoners saw an enormous concrete arch scattered with vertical reinforcing rods. The large clearing area appeared towering. A massive half-cylindrical concrete structure stood above them , eight hundred feet long, two hundred and seventy feet wide, and some ninety-five feet high. Under the glaring floodlights, cranes and bulldozers swarmed the area. Fifteen thousand men worked around the clock, monitored in groups of thirty. They pushed small wagons and carried concrete and building materials. Prisoners stood on platforms handling large hoses and carrying fifty to hundred pound sacks of cement towards spiked grid work. Other inmates moved about with metal equipment and buckets, distributing wet cement and smoothing the area with their shovels. They collected gravel and fed the dirt to huge mixers. Thousands of men in striped uniforms ran in and out of the compound carrying lumber and iron rods from the railroad tracks that stood at the entrance of the construction site.[232]

This was Moll. This colossal structure was built to assist the German air force. Allied forces had bombed several airplane factories in Germany. Low on ME 262 Messerschmitt planes, the German government contracted with the Leohnard Moll construction firm ("Moll" as the inmates referred to it) to build a bombproof base, concealed from aerial view, to store an arsenal of these fighter planes. To assist with the war effort, and especially to make profits, the administrators of the Leohnard Moll construction firm bought Kaufering inmates daily to work at the construction site.[233]

AT FIVE A.M.

The prisoners, again, marched four miles to Moll. The inmates labored, moving in a steady rhythm, calmly digging and carrying the cement so as not to overstrain themselves. "Move faster! Much faster," the German guard threatened, "this is no place for laziness! Continue with your work, or the devil will get you. If you do not complete your duty, you will be sent to hell."[234] Ukrainian prisoners spoke in their native tongue. Machine operators yelled in German. Thousands of Jews from Poland, Lithuania, and Hungary installed gridwork as they spoke to each other in Yiddish.[235]

With Jews as well as gentiles originating from different parts of Europe, the inmates had difficulty communicating with one another. Prisoners simply could not find the words or hand motions to convey their wants. Limited in speech, laboring in an environment that looked more like the tower of Babel than an industrial worksite, the prisoners tried to focus on their designated tasks, lifting hundred pound bags of cement, forming iron rods and transporting industrial equipment from the trains towards the worksite.[236] The prisoners who labored on the upper stories of Moll were especially prone to workplace injury. Confused about their duties and the ground slippery, inmates often lost their footing. A prisoner fell some one hundred feet, hitting the bars and concrete on the floor level. The mangled corpse landed on the iron reinforcements. The Capo and the German officers ordered that the body should remain where it lay.[237] They told the workers to pour cement over the corpse.[238] "Another Jew is dead," they retorted, "continue with your work, more will come from Auschwitz."[239]

* * *

Over the next few weeks, slave labor and the lack of proper nourishment began to take its toll. Hundreds of inmates began to die from exhaustion.[240] When a Jewish slave died from fatigue and starvation, Moll operators took day workers and assigned them to the twelve-hour night shift. They later ordered new inmates from Auschwitz.[241] The Nazis, too, did not care about the prisoners. The desire to support their depleting armies in the short term was more important than maintaining prisoners for long term gain. Time was of the essence for the Germans even if increasing production meant decimating their labor force.[242]

There was no gas chamber in Kaufering. And there was no need for one. Jewish slaves simply expired from starvation, abuse, and working long hours at Moll. The inmates labored continuously while the guards monitored with their rifles. They struck prisoners in the ribs if they did not have enough cement in their shovels.[243] The Germans decreed, "Death through Work," while the inmates cried "The sword is worse than death, famine is worse than the sword, and imprisonment is worst of all."[244]

Dachau – Kaufering

Nationality – *Lithuanian;* **Race** – *Jewish;* **Height** – *170 cm;* **Language** – *Jewish (Yiddish), Lithuanian, and German;* **Hair** – *black;* **Face** – *circular;* **Teeth** – *normal,* **Nose** – *normal,* **Mouth** – *normal. Arrested on August 15, 1941 for preventive measures. Admitted to Kaufering on July 29, 1944.*[245]

The Germans neatly examined every bone and facial feature, cleverly confirming their racial theories and pseudo-science. He has the smell of a Jew, the nose of a Jew. Like the rest of them, he is a thief, a loafer, the parasite who lives at the expense of others.[246]

Leib understood this to be his life. He would have to labor at Moll, feed large iron bars into metal bending machines, and hold the rods in place until it formed the proper shape.[247] He would have to manage with the three hundred grams of bread and watery vegetable soup.

A few weeks after arriving in the camp, he explained to a registration official that he was a roofer, a practical job that would give the Germans the impression that he was valuable. The register then gave him a number – 85004 – and sewed this number onto his uniform below the yellow star.[248]

It was the end of a cool summer

One evening, after he returned from Moll, Leib noticed some

shrubs sprouting on the other side of the fence. He came closer to get a better look and recognized potato tubers just beginning to bloom.

Leib planned to switch to Moll's night shift. Perhaps then, at night, when everyone came back from work, he would be able to make his way to the potato patch.[249] Workers despised the night assignment. They labored for eleven hours at Moll, from sundown to sunrise, in five degrees Fahrenheit weather. For Leib, though, switching to the night shift gave him the opportunity to walk around the camp more easily. After the workers made their way back from Moll at four a.m., he would have the chance to slip away to the tubers.

Leib slowly walked around the fence, avoiding the sentries and dodging the headlights. As he walked along the edge of the camp, he found a small hole in the ground near the fence. He dug a little for himself, snuck past the first and then past the second fence.[250] Leib found the potato tubers. They were just beginning to make their way to the ground's surface. He picked a few of the tubers, put some in his mouth, and took the rest back to the camp. After returning, Leib dug a hole in the ground next to his barrack and hid the extra tubers in the dirt.[251]

Each night that he collected tubers at the patch, he buried the extra food in this hole. When his tubers ran low, he went to a garbage pit behind the German kitchen. In the midst of the dirty water and refuse, there lay some food scraps, some *shalach* as he referred to it, and he searched through the filth and fluid to find a few potato peels.[252]

* * *

A few weeks after locating the potato fields, Leib noticed that other inmates were taking his tubers. He gathered and replenished his hole consistently. Now the tubers were gone.[253] At Moll the next day, Leib approached a German prisoner who made bricks.

Being of a superior race, the German owned a locker where he stored food and other essentials. Leib asked the brick-maker if he could use the locker for storage. The German agreed but only in exchange for some tubers. The terms were reached, the symbiotic relationship established. Leib kept his food in the German locker, free from the hands of other prisoners, and he gave the brick-maker a percentage of his potatoes.[254]

Leib smuggled, stored, traded, and apportioned scraps of food.[255] Two slices of bread for a bowl of soup, half a potato for some leftover cheese, carrots for a few Marks, a cigarette for two potatoes. He still looked skinny and decrepit. His muscles slowly atrophied. Yet, relative to the hundreds of malnourished prisoners, he appeared healthy. Throughout the camp and especially among the Capos at Moll, he was known as the *grober* – the fat one.[256]

FALL 1944

Leib worked in the cold at the eleven-hour night shift. He bent metal bars used as the base for Moll's floor.[257] The Capo who monitored Leib's group walked away from his position for a few seconds. With a few frozen potatoes in his pocket, Leib ran from the worksite, darting up a hill towards a large pile of dirt. The area was perfect. In the darkest part of the night, behind the huge mound of dirt, the Capos and the German guards would never see him consume the potatoes. This time, however, was different. "Stay put! Stay where you are prisoner. Stay put!" Leib looked over the mound and recognized a German quickly moving in his direction. The guard shouted multiple times, cocking his rifle back as he ran up the hill. Leib dropped the potatoes and ran towards the guard. Sprinting towards the officer as fast he could with his arms held forward, he pushed the guard down the hill. Leib ran back to the worksite and continued his work with the rest of the inmates.

The German who rolled down the hill searched for Leib throughout Moll. He inspected the brigades, asking each Capo if they had seen a young prisoner. But it was the darkest part of night. The guard could not accurately describe him. Among the mass of bald heads and black and white clothes, the administrators at Moll never found the prisoner who had the gumption to push a German down a hill.[258]

"I have been saved by miracles in the past. I can move forward this time as well. I will not accept my current situation," Leib thought, "I will find means, a way to better my circumstances. Potatoes are on the outside; a way to better my diet is through food and trade. There are means, there are ways, I will find them." Despite the oppressors' cruelty, his determination kept him healthy. Who is rich? There is no wealth in Kaufering. Who can survive? He who is not satisfied with his lot.[259]

It was October 1944

Things had never been worse. Hard work combined with malnutrition and the dropping temperature was taking its toll. One foot stood in the camp, the other in the next world. The prisoners' eyelids and legs began to swell. Extreme weight loss followed. Some of the inmates walked around the yard, their legs appearing like two twigs, their hips protruding inward. They slowly completed their duties as if they had just woken up from a deep sleep. They made their way from Moll to Kaufering, labored at the worksite, transported the dead to pits outside of the camp, and mumbled their words.

Concerned only with hunger pains, the *Musselmanner,* as they were called, performed their work in a torpid like state. With their emaciated cheeks and bony features, the *Musselmanner* appeared as if they were not of this world. They were "walking skeletons," "skeletons covered with skin," "ghosts of humanity".[260] Some *Musselmanners* died in their bunks. Some were sent to the back of the kitchen without food to expire. Others were transported to Auschwitz to perish in the gas chambers.

With the end of Winter

The mundane became essential. Shoes and clean clothes became critical for survival. Storage became as valuable as water, fitted shoes as important as food, and a clean shirt as valuable as shelter. The problem of shoes struck Leib first. He marched down the muddy road for seven miles, back and forth from Kaufering to Moll. The wooden clogs from Stutthof never seemed to fit. He was last everywhere. The soles scrubbed against his ankles and the arch of his foot. After eight weeks of making the trip to Moll, his feet were bruised and his legs became swollen.

On his return from Moll one day, Leib saw a Lithuanian Jew making shoes. The man put his foot on a wooden board that he took from Moll, outlined its shape, cut the area, and nailed the wooden board to the straps.

"That was relatively simple," Leib thought, "I could do this just as well." Leib then followed the Lithuanian shoemaker's example. He outlined his foot on a wooden board, used a knife to cut around the outline and nailed the wooden board to leather straps.[261]

Clean clothes became another necessity for survival. Every prisoner understood the seriousness of this. The abysmal sanitary condition at Kaufering, lacking the means to clean themselves, and never changing their underwear, made the invasion of lice almost inevitable. By September 1944, most of the prisoners at Kaufering were covered in lice. Prison shirts and caps teemed with layers of lice, their garb transmuting from shades of black to gray to white.

Prisoners spent many hours shaking lice off their clothing. They sat on the edge of their wooden bunks picking off the lice from their uniforms and crushing them between their fingers. Leib and some of the other prisoners lit the makeshift stove in the middle of the bunk, turned their garments inside out and shook their clothes over the flames. The lice would return a few days later. The prisoners repeated the process. By winter, the lice began to increase and typhus, a disease carried by lice, spread throughout the camp.[262]

* * *

The cold air ran through the prisoners' bones. With temperatures ranging from five to negative five degrees Fahrenheit, the inmates pulled the blankets off their beds and wrapped them around their bodies. Leib took a rag to Moll so that he could grab the bars without his hands freezing when he touched the iron. After a few weeks, Leib stole a cement bag from Moll and cut out a half circle on the top for his neck and two holes on the sides for his arms. He then cut up the extra pieces and stuck the material deep into his shoes, hidden from the S.S..[263]

The winter was unbearable for many. On some days, up to fifteen people died. The corpses lay on the bare expanse like dung on the open field. When all the inmates left for Moll or another worksite, the block leaders and the *Musselmen* delivered the bodies to the camp gate. They loaded the dead on frozen hand carts and dumped the corpses into a large ditch behind the camp. By January 1945, the Germans replaced the dying population with hundreds of prisoners from Auschwitz. The recent arrivals, mostly Polish Jews, wore torn prisoner garb and stood outside, shaking back and forth from the cold. These new arrivals stripped the dead of their clothing unconcerned about the possible infection of cholera or typhus. They were only worried about keeping warm.[264]

* * *

With the weather conditions getting chillier each day, the Capos and their German superiors hammered the prisoners even more. The beatings were especially vicious after a German loss.[265] One day, two Germans stood on either side of Leib and began striking him with their batons. Leib ran and managed to escape a few feet. One guard caught up to him and whacked him again. Leib ran back the other way while the second guard grabbed him and beat him with a rod. As he ran from the two guards, he started screaming to get the attention of civilians working outside the camp. The laborers watched the scene for a while. They assembled, staring at Leib as he ran from one guard to the other. Afraid of attracting witnesses, the two officers finally let Leib go.[266]

FEBRUARY AND MARCH, 1945

For the prisoners at Kaufering, starvation rations continued. Leib just blew on the bread and like a dandelion half of it disappeared. Sprinkled with sawdust and mold, the bread disintegrated after a few days.[267] Leib told a story of how he obtained food from an acquaintance:

> About three months before I was liberated, there was nothing to eat... nothing. An acquaintance came to me and said: "I have, you know, a sheep's head." The prisoner asked me if I wanted to buy this sheep's head for five Marks. I used to go out in the fields at night to look for potatoes, and I used to sell the potatoes. So, I had a little bit of money, not a lot, but a little bit.[268]
>
> "Let me see the sheep head," I asked. He showed me and I saw that the sheep was barking (laughing). It was a dog's head. And, I bought it.
>
> I will tell you; you don't understand what hunger means. Those born here [in the United States] can't understand this. I went to the German kitchen where all the dirty water, everything from the kitchen, and maybe from the toilet too, used to go into a big pit. I used to go fishing. I made myself a little can, with a big stick, and put it into about ten feet [of water]. I found some frozen potatoes that the

> Germans had thrown out, wiped off the dirt and took off the peels. I remember this. I then skinned the dog's head, took out the meat and cooked the potatoes with it. And you know it was very good. I was a lucky man to get it.[269]

Rotten food, ridden with dirt and feces, Leib consumed anything that he could get his hands on. Dog or sheep, it all could be digested.

* * *

With his poor diet and lack of vitamin C, Leib contracted scurvy. He experienced shortness of breath and his teeth started to rot. Some of his front teeth fell out. As a last resort, Leib checked himself into the camp hospital and spent a week recuperating.[270] Then, almost at random, rumors circulated throughout the camp that the Red Cross planned to send food packages to the inmates. Among the prisoners, the news of Red Cross packages was merely a cruel joke.[271] It was fodder for the cynic, another false hope that people actually cared about their condition. But in the middle of March 1945 the packages came. Prisoners would receive either a little can of sardines or a small bag of sugar.

Before the Germans distributed the packages, Leib and another inmate made a pact. "If I get the sugar I will share it with you," Leib said, "and if you get the sugar you will share it with me." The inmates wanted the sugar since it could be rationed. The packages came. Everyone held their parcels tightly, clasping it in their fingers like a precious stone.[272] Leib received the sugar; his acquaintance received sardines. It was late in the war. Every passing day with food improved his chance at survival. Yet, he promised to split the sugar, and he kept his word.

Leib utilized every piece of sugar. He took a little bit each day and touched it to the tip of his tongue. He did the same the next and every day afterward for the next two weeks.[273]

The need for food was desperate. Slowly, Leib was becoming a *Musselman*. By the end of March 1945, he progressively lost weight. One hundred. Eighty. Finally, seventy pounds.[274] Starvation was taking its toll. As the days passed, Leib and the rest of the prisoners slowly began to sink into a dream world rather than face reality.[275] Leib carried the cement bags and formed the iron bars for Moll's floor. He waited at the *Appellplatz* in the cold for hours. But it was too much. He started daydreaming. He had reminisced about his father's murder time and again. Perhaps on this occasion as well, the image of his father, lying in the Seventh Fort in the throes of death, came to mind. "This is Torah," he remembered saying. He reached for his father's *tallis katan*, but it was drenched in blood. "This is Torah and this is its reward," he said.

There was once a great Jewish Sage named Elisha ben Avuyah. He was an expert in Jewish law and a man of character. He was the teacher of Rabbi Meir. Yet, Elisha could not tolerate the slaughter of his people. Children murdered. Wives kidnapped from husbands. A great conflagration ran throughout the alleys of Jerusalem and in the outside provinces. Water could not quench it, rivers could not flood it.[276] It encircled the wooden homes and blackened the stone. The fire spread through the villages and towards the ruins of the Temple Mount. It blazed through the streets and into the heart of Elisha ben Avuyah. Elisha's anguishing spirit cried out. His faith burned along with the fire that had consumed the righteous. "This is Torah and this is its reward." After seeing the tongue of a Torah scholar dragged through the streets by a pig, he exclaimed, "The mouth that uttered pearls of Torah now licks the dust," and he separated himself from the ways of Torah.[277]

Leib could not reject the faith of his youth. He needed to embrace it. A feeling of pleasantness came upon him just by verbalizing the word "Torah." It brought him closer. From his own being, the Torah drew him in. "Continue," it calls, "continue in your studies with the same vigor and determination as before.

Elisha ben Avuya's legacy has not died; he has lived on through his student, Rabbi Meir." He is the continuation. "Where Elisha had failed, Meir has succeeded. Where Elisha relinquished belief in Providence, Rabbi Meir has affirmed it." Rabbi Meir asked, "What distinguishes *techelet*, the blue string that aligned the fringes of one's *tallis katan*, from all other types of dyes? Because the color of *techelet* is similar to the sea, and the sea is similar to the sky, and the sky is similar to G-d's Throne of Glory."[278] When a person looks at the sea, he knows with complete certainty that there is life beneath the water. Even though when one looks at the surface he only sees blue, he knows with certainty that there is life below the ocean floor. So too, when one looks at the sky, even though one cannot see Him, a Jew should know with certainty that G-d is in Heaven.[279]

Where is the Lord, the G-d of Elijah?[280] Where is His presence now that everything has been destroyed? Where is the clean *tallis katan*, white and black? The sky is similar to the Throne of Glory. I know that He is with me.

In the midst of his daydreaming, a Capo marched over to him. "You see this hand?" he said. Leib suddenly awoke. The Capo extended his fingers wide and with all his force, smacked Leib in the head. "Wake up!" the guard yelled as Leib crashed to the dirt.[281]

On April 24th, 1945

The Germans announced that all prisoners at Kaufering would leave the camp. Everybody, except for those in the camp hospital, had to gather their rations and line up at the *Appellplatz*. Confusion and panic rose among the inmates. Should they follow orders and be lead by their captors? Should they stay back with the ill? The Russians were already on the outskirts of Berlin, the Americans a few days away from Kaufering. Leib ran to the central square.[282]

The March

The disheveled ran out of the barracks; the *Musselmanner* joined the ranks. Two thousand prisoners marched out of Kaufering, moving towards Dachau, in groups of a hundred.[283] Red Cross vans followed the prisoners. The inmates entered Dachau proper. Leib saw more Red Cross personnel mingling with the Germans. The Capos gave the prisoners some soup and a bit of bread, and again the Germans ordered the prisoners to march. Two thousand prisoners walked southwards in the direction of the Bavarian mountains. For two days, Leib and the group marched in the cold. They walked past houses and some empty farms. A few grabbed the sprouts and grass that stood on the side of the street. Some collapsed on the side of the road.[284]

By late April, 1945

The Americans were making their way into Southern Germany. Shots could be heard a few miles away. Everyone – especially the guards – knew this. Their eyes revealed it all. They only monitored the prisoners so they would not have to engage in battle.[285] Leib patiently scanned the foremen and searched for someone who might help.[286] "The eyes are the windows to the soul," he thought as he studied each officer's face. "Maybe now, in their time of fear, the guards will show some leniency and allow me to escape."[287] After looking at a few German guards, Leib found his man. He asked the German officer if he could go to the bushes and defecate on the side of the road. The German allowed him to do this. Leib pulled down his pants and waited a few minutes for the rest of the group to pass. With a rifle in his hand, the guard continued to monitor the prisoner. It was just the German and Leib now. The brigade a few feet up the road, Leib pulled up his pants and walked away. The German guard ran back towards the rest of the group, unconcerned about Leib.[288]

Leib continued, walking away from the roads, heading towards the vast stretches of farmland. In one of the properties he came upon, Leib heard a young boy and girl playing outside. He moved closer and spied on the children from a distance. After a few minutes, Leib made his way over. Though horrified by the sight of the prisoner, the children hesitantly walked towards Leib. From his atrophied muscles to his despondent appearance, the children understood what the starving inmate needed. They ran into the house to fetch some fruit and water. The children's father came out to see the prisoner too. Sympathetic at the sight of the inmate, the farmer allowed Leib to sleep in their barn.[289][290]

Bullets and artillery shots could be heard outside. The Americans came closer to Munich, marching past the crops and the rich farmland. Leib ran to the window to look at these men. Were they foreign occupiers, other guards who would show cruelty and indifference? They were soldiers with weapons in their hands after all. Yet among the battalion, Leib saw a friendly face. He ran outside to see the soldier in person. It was an American soldier with the letters Cincinnati sown onto the front of his uniform. As Leib approached the man, the soldier pulled out a Hebrew prayer book to show him that he was a Jew. Leib told the solider in

Yiddish about the two thousand prisoners marching towards the Bavarian Alps, and the solider promised him that his unit would free the inmates.[291]

Was this happening? Was Leib also free? Leib grabbed the soldier, half wondering if this was real or just another dream. They shared a common bond, they were both Jewish. And, now, they shared another bond – they were both free men.

Recovery

The gates of tears are never locked.

- Baba Metzia 59a

Blood has been spilled, Jewish blood. It flowed in streams through Kovno and Germany. The wicked have walked on every side, baseness has been exalted among men. Yet, what can the righteous do? What power do they have now that all of European Jewry has been decimated?[292] Leib was consumed with such questions:

> After the terrible destruction that took place during the Holocaust, what can we say happened to the Jewish people? Thousands, millions of Jews, our dearest and beloved ones, were burnt in a large fire that the world ignited upon us. In the Talmud it is written, "The gates of tears are never locked."[293] Though all gates may be closed for us, the gates of tears are always open. No other thing can do so much as tears.[294]

So, with tears in their eyes, the survivors – the *She'erith Hapleitah*, as they called themselves – mourned over their relatives. They reflected on their experiences in the camps, their grief hanging in a shadow of darkness. The recollections of murder and torture were not loose memory, but a repeated scene, scalded into their consciousness. During this time, Leib wrote the following poem:[295]

Nekamah [Revenge]

Kol Demei Acheinu Tzoakim Aleinu Min Ha'Adamah

[The bloodied voice of our brothers cry to us from the earth!]

A whole column of Jews are going, and they go, as we understand now, to death.

Soon, I will have to give away my life without a reason, without a "Why?" and without a "For What?"

My dear child is crying.

What does this innocent baby, this innocent little creature know?

Soon, soon is our end.

How can earth and heaven witness my pain and be silent?

The world is so corrupt!

I continue on my way, and I already see the long dug pits.

Yes, here will soon be my naked child's and my cold body.

The hangmen ordered, "All get undressed!"

I begin to undress my child and at the same time myself.

The clothes are put in order and I cuddle my child against my chest.

I begin to scream – Why?

Why have I earned this?

Why should such a barbaric things be done and the world is not reacting?

Is it only because I am a Jew? And, therefore, there is no "Why?"

And so, while complaining "Why?" one can hear the sound of a machine gun and a mother falling into the pit together with "Why?" on her lips.

The child remains, witnessing it.

This is what you have for your "Why?"

The hangman comes soon to the child.

He picks up the child on his bayonet and throws him into the pit.

The child is buried alive.

Yes, parents are dead, brothers and sisters are dead, but some of the children did survive, and they have to continue the "Why?"

First, we have to complain to the entire world: Why?

Why was the world silent when we were killed? Why?

Why did they allow them to do this and why, even today, do they still allow them? Why?
Why, after the Holocaust, after millions were killed, do they continue to leave people in the camps?

Why don't they let us go to our Land?

Why are Jews beaten even now?

That is the first "Why?" from parents, brothers and sisters in the last minute of their lives.

But now, after the Holocaust, we have a new "Why?"

There is a new Holocaust, and again the world is not listening to any "Why?"

So now is the end of our call –
Demei Acheinu Tzoakim Aleinu Min Ha'Adamah – Nekamah
[The blood of our brothers cry out to us from the earth – revenge].[296]

Even with liberation

The death toll did not end. Some thirty thousand people, with no clothes, malnourished and exposed to typhus and cholera, passed away after liberation. Many died from their chronic maladies. Others from the psychological trauma of their new found freedom.[297] In early May, while Leib's marching group was being liberated, Leib entered a makeshift hospital in west Germany located in a monastery called St. Ottilien.

Former inmates from Dachau and Buchenwald sought care at St. Ottilien. Carrying a few belongings in wagons and wheeling the sick in carriages, hundreds of survivors searched throughout western Germany for medical care. They wandered in the countryside and in the main cities in striped pajamas with knapsacks on their shoulders. Like homeless peasants, they slept on the streets, avoiding the Germans, eating whatever scraps they could barter or find on the road.[298]

St. Ottilien was a Jewish refuge, a hospital as well as a gathering place for Jews. Thousands of Jews, whether originally from Greece, Hungary, Poland, Slovakia, and Lithuania, rallied around its grounds. The patients slept a few inches away from one another. They lay on two chairs placed next to each other, mattresses on the floor, or a wooden board. Leib was lucky to find space at the hospital. He had been liberated a few days earlier than the survivors on the march and obtained a bed. Malnourished, fatigued, his lower thighs and ankles swollen, the doctors at St. Ottilien diagnosed Leib with poor blood circulation as well as irregular breathing.[299]

The survivors were not the only ones at St. Ottilien. Germans and former Capos also came to to the monastery to find medical care. They walked through the corridors of St. Ottilien as if they had committed no crimes and as if the atrocities at Kaufering had never occurred.

After a few months, Leib's symptoms improved and he became a guard at St. Ottilien.[300] He walked along the monastery grounds, guarding the residents from potential burglars. One day, Leib recognized the Capo who had hit him with his open palm. It had just been a few months ago, and Leib easily recognized him. He notified the other guards and urged them to join. "You see this palm," Leib exclaimed as he tapped the Capo on his shoulder. Leib slammed his palm into the man's nose just as the Capo had done some months before. The other men began to beat the former guard.[301]

It did not matter – Lithuanian, German, Capo – the survivors wanted to take revenge on the Germans and anyone who assisted them. Memories of these perpetrators almost maddened the survivors. It haunted their dreams and engulfed their senses. They engraved the word *nekamah* on their walls and formed groups to take retaliation on the Germans.[302] Most Jews, however, decided on a more symbolic revenge. They separated themselves from the perpetrators, created families in the Land of Israel, and privately derided Germany. Casting the German people as a genocidal nation with no standing in the world, a people who could never destroy world Jewry, was more satisfying than physical retribution.[303]

For the next few months

Leib stayed at St. Ottilien while his health improved. In December 1945, the doctors of St. Ottilien discharged Leib because the hospital had to reorganize itself.[304] The doctors needed space to accommodate more serious cases and in order to do so, the hospital staff discharged Leib.

Leib traveled to Munich. He bartered with Germans for the next few weeks and planned to immigrate to the Land of Israel. However, Leib's health kept regressing. On January 25, 1946, he returned to St. Ottilien, suffering from bronchitis.[305] He spent a few days recovering from this illness. On February 6, 1946, the doctors at St. Ottilien discharged Leib a second time.[306] Leib moved around Munich with some other survivors, trading small goods to survive.[307] He continued this for the next few months. In April, 1946, as boats left from Italy to the Land of Israel, Leib, along with some twelve hundred survivors made their way south towards Rome.[308] For the next three months, he moved from one D.P. camp to another in order to get closer to the ships leaving for the Land of Israel.[309]

May 1946

At a D.P. camp in Rome, Leib came into contact with a group of Jews illegally immigrating to the Land of Israel.[310] The band specialized in such ventures and the group's administrators placed Leib in a unit that would secretly sail to the Holy Land. Leib marched to the Roman harbor, and British officers followed his unit. With the police trailing, other, more politically acceptable Jews, walked towards another dock where they boarded a ship. Leib's group, on the other hand, remained in Italy. In the upcoming months, the band's administrators manipulated Leib multiple times.

"We all had a dream to move to our Land," Leib later reported, but the people who had promised him emigration "were liars."[311] Leib had little standing. He was a *yatom*, an orphan, with little contacts. Leib headed back to Germany, forced to give up his dream of moving to the Land of Israel.[312]

LEIB TRAVELED TO FRANCE

Eventually, Leib settled in Bailly, a small French suburb with a small Jewish population. The Jews who settled in Bailly used the area as a stopover before immigrating to the United States and Israel. Most of them came to Bailly with this intention.[313]

Refugees of all ages came to Bailly: Polish couples who fled to Russia before the German invasion, Russian Jews from the Soviet Union, former yeshivah students and their families, and some Lithuanian and Polish survivors of the *Shoah*. With the assistance of the Joint Distribution Committee, these refugees rented a château on a large, green hill overlooking the Palace of Versailles.[314]

Refugees flocked to the area to receive housing and support before emigration. They completed paperwork and waited for visas that would allow them to emigrate. The Jews at Bailly used the château for educational purposes as well. They established a *yeshivah ketana*, consisting of about sixty boys, and a *yeshivah gedola* of about fifty young men.[315] They named these institutions under the umbrella name, *Yeshivoth Reunis* – The Yeshivas Uniting the *She'erith Hapleitah* of Poland and Lithuania.

Due to no fault of their own, the yeshivah was poorly organized. The student body consisted of students of different ages. Some had just turned Bar Mitzvah, others were in their twenties and thirties. Class sizes continuously fluctuated since students quickly emigrated as soon as they received a visa.[316] Yet despite its haphazard composition, the Bailly yeshivah became a focal point for the community. Residents became custodians and janitors for the yeshivah. Some shipped food and cooked for the students. Others became administrators and teachers, continuing their pedagogic duties as they had done in the pre-war yeshivas in the towns of Telz and Novardok. While learning in the yeshivah, Leib worked for the Joint Distribution Committee completing paperwork and transporting food to the Jewish community. He spoke with French officials and arranged visas for residents at the château.

* * *

Teachers at the Bailly yeshivah attempted to transplant the old way of learning into their new environment. Many teachers taught their students *mussar*, a Lithuanian educational program which emphasized conscious devotion to G-d and ethical development. Most prominently among the teachers was Rabbi Mordechai (Mottel) Pagramanski, a recognized genius in Lithuania. Rabbi Pagramanski spent much of his day learning Torah. In the Kovno Ghetto, Rabbi Pagramanski remained in hiding, absorbed in his thoughts, studying the Torah without any texts.[317] After the War, he spent his nights immersed in his books, waking up sporadically, reportedly seventeen times, to return to his studies. He amended the text of the Medieval Talmudic commentator, Rabbi Yom Tov ben Avraham, whose writings contained printing mistakes.

Rabbi Pagramanski was a mysterious man, known for his genius and his ascetic behavior. He separated himself from the material world, neglecting his physical needs in the pursuit of Torah scholarship.[318] Some Jews at Bailly, including Leib, assisted the Rabbi financially and with his daily tasks.[319] It was an honor to help the man, as many believed him to be the greatest Sage in post-war Europe, reminiscent of the Gaon of Vilna.

Rabbi Pagramanski provided administrators with advice. He educated students as well as laymen, considering many current issues. He interpreted problems critically and from a psychological perspective.[320] Following *mussar* principles, Rabbi Pagramanski empathized with others, concerning himself with the student's education as well as their spiritual well-being. The full breadth of his personality and teachings, however, were cut short. In 1949, Rabbi Pagramanski passed away from cancer.[321]

* * *

Leib developed a close bond with another yeshivah supervisor, Rabbi Chaim Leib Zacks, the former community Rabbi of Uzdah. Rabbi Zacks was a decider of Jewish law. A master of Talmud and codes, he exhibited confidence in his scholarship, his breadth of knowledge, and his *halakhic* rulings. It was Rabbi Zacks, more so than Rabbi Pagramanski, who influenced Leib. The two learned Talmud together in Bailly and later on in the United States where both men studied in the Telz Yeshivah in Cleveland.[322] Leib shared many of Rabbi Zack's principles and received rabbinic ordination from him at the yeshivah in Bailly.

The flame of the Lithuanian yeshivot had dimmed. Those mighty houses of learning had been burned to ash. Many students had passed on, their families left behind. Yet the few who remained had never given up hope. In the wayward countries of France and the United States, in the fledgling State of Israel, the fire of Torah continued to burn. The yeshivot destroyed in Lithuania sprang to life once more.[323]

* * *

At a wedding in Paris, Leib met a man named Rabbi Yitzhak Itzikovitz. A Lithuanian Jew himself, Yitzhak liked the young survivor and invited him to his home. For the next few years, Leib became part of the Itzikovitz household. Many passed through the Itzikovitz house to collect food and find residence before they left for the United States and Israel. Leib remained. He came to the Itzikovitz's home almost every day to use their stove and facilities. He asked Yitzhak advice about a proper profession, Torah, and about life in general.[324] After much effort and perseverance, Leib married Yitzhak's daughter, Esther, a few years later.

THE MEMORIES AND HORRORS

The Holocaust would always remain with Leib. It would haunt his dreams, fill his conversation, and oftentimes, consume his present reality. "When I go speak of this [the *Grosse Aktion*]," Leib explained, "I can see everything."[325] He recalled his mother Chiene, his father Yitzhak, and his six brothers and sisters. He remembered the innocent who had perished, where the straight were obliterated, and, the potential of the righteous whose lives were cut short.[326]

> My mother was forty years old when she died. When people grow old, naturally, it is [a blessing]. For our people its a big thing to die from old age for most were killed young... They were young lives [and] they cut them off. Terrible. Six million, a million and a half children. Can you imagine this? – doctors, scientists, and scholars. I will tell you something, if we were to stop and think what we went through, it is unbelievable for ourselves to say I went through this.[327]

Leib was one of a handful of Lithuanian Jews who made it out of the ghetto and escaped Kaufering. With the aid of the native population, the Germans annihilated ninety-four percent of Lithuanian Jewry – over two hundred and forty-three thousand Jews.[328] Of those who came under direct Nazi control, only one percent survived.[329]

For Leib, his survival came about through a mixture of decisive action and Providence. "I know myself," Leib recalled, "I was heading for death so many times. It was just because I fought for this [that I survived]. If I would tell these stories.... miracles." It was a mixture of the two, man standing with his feet planted on the ground *mi darf fighten,* fighting for his bread and his life, with the confidence that G-d will help.[330]

* * *

The more time passed, the more the survivor judged himself unfavorably. The man of the camp never forgot his experience, but considered his decisions under Nazi rule with disdain. "If I were to go through the *Grosse Aktion* now I would have known what to do and save the family," Leib said in his Los Angeles home in 1988. "At the time I just ran away from them."

"I should have saved my brother," he so often repeated. This feeling of regret stood with him as an emotional scar that could not be cured with logic. Logic can only alleviate problems of the mind. It cannot treat pains of the heart.

Despite living through the worst of the diaspora, Leib believed that G-d was with him. After liberation, there was a gentle push to continue in his faith and the Torah of his youth. He longed for G-d. And as he persisted in the study of Torah and the performance of the commandments, the encouragement from Him became all the more stronger.

Leib witnessed the murder of his family and the decimation of his community. He felt the reality of his traumatic past but accepted the unknowables of His ways. He accepted the plan set out for him from the beginning – when the world was filled with water.

Belief, faith in G-d, was a palpable force, visible to those who heard him speak. From his confident tone to the expressive sound of his words, one could see how trust in G-d was entrenched to his inner being. He often said:

> When I see everything in this world, I know there is a G-d. Man can make from something, something, but only G-d can make from nothing, something. I know there is a Power. I cannot see it, but I can feel it. And I know that when I pray to Him, He is answering my prayers.

Epilogue

Remember what Amalek did. He ambushed and struck the weakest. He did not fear G-d. It shall be when Hashem allows the nation to rest from all this torment, the Jewish people shall wipe out the memory of Amalek.[331] Destroy the eternal enemy of the Jewish people, the nation of Amalek. Take revenge on those whom he slaughtered. Yet, after thousands of years, the Jewish people do not know who Amalek is. Is Amalek a particular people or is the call for their destruction simply theoretical?

The survivors of the *Shoah* also called out in revenge against the Germans and their collaborators. "The blood of our brothers cry out to us from the earth – revenge." It was a literal call. The survivors wanted retribution for their ravaged communities and their relatives who were murdered. It was a call of familial loss and of personal suffering. This was just as true for Leib as it was for many in the displaced person's camps. These men and women spoke of their lonesome misfortune and unbearable torment. "How can heaven and earth witness my pain and be silent?"[332]

Revenge never dissipated. These feelings settled in the bottom of the survivor's mind and filled his thoughts at random moments. As time passed, the call for revenge changed. It went from a scream to a cry. What could I do to take revenge? Could I take the lives of the perpetrators and their families? Surely not. For most of the survivors believed that they could never sink to the murderers' level. Just as the Torah's call for the literal destruction of Amalek became theoretical, so their call for revenge became, in their state of limitations, theoretical.[333]

* * *

With the help of the Telz Yeshivah in Cleveland, Leib moved to the United States on February 15th, 1951 on board the ship "Liberte".[334] He learned in Yeshivat Telz. One day, he wrote a letter to Esther Itzikovitz, asking her to to join him in the United States. She agreed and moved to Cleveland. A few months later, Esther and Leib got married.[335]

Leib was trying to create a family with Esther, to rebuild and move forward. He spent many hours working as a *shochet* [a ritual slaughterer], providing for his wife and three children. There was no time to be consumed with anger.[336] Still, he conversed. He spoke of the past, about the suffering he went through, and the strength of the Kovno community that had been forgotten. He spoke of the Torah, learned in his youth and after the war. These two themes, the *Shoah* and Torah, filled his conversations with both family and strangers alike. Horror and light, it was his daily speech. In his later years, when he was free from the worries of financially supporting his family, he spoke more. The call for revenge slowly lessened. It was only a prayer.

OCTOBER 28, 1984

The house is dimly lit. The paint drips from the walls. Clean tables line the room where a few Lithuanian Jews, survivors and escapees from the Holocaust, wait for the next speaker. Leib gets up from his chair and slowly walks to the center of the room. I have flourished, he thinks. My tent is at peace and in my home nothing is amiss.[337] Thank G-d, I am blessed with a loving wife, three children, and two grandchildren.[338] They sit around me almost like grass in the field.[339] Still, this obligation falls upon me. I must speak up. I must say a few words about an earlier generation. I must prepare myself for an investigation about our fathers.[340]

Dear Lithuanian Jews:

We are assembled here today to mark the memory of our precious fathers and mothers, brothers and sisters. Exactly forty-three years ago today, on the 28th of October, 1941, the *Grosse Aktion* of the Kovno Ghetto took place. Who among us can forget it? That terrible day, when the murderers, the Germans and Lithuanians *yemach shemam*, tore away twelve thousand Jews – men, women, and children – to shoot them at the Ninth Fort.

The Torah tells us about the tragedy of Aharon's two sons; they were burned by G-d. The Torah says, *Va'yidom Aharon* – and Aharon was silent.[341] After such a tragedy, at a time that a father has to bury his children, Aharon became almost paralyzed; he was without words. The Torah states later on, "*V'acheichem Bnei Yisrael yibchu et haserefa asher saraf Hashem* – And their brothers, the House of Israel, should mourn over the fire which G-d burned."[342]

The Torah required *Bnei Yisrael* to mourn for just two Jewish children. Today, precious Jews, in that place, they led out twelve thousandJews – men, women, and children – undressed them completely and drove them into the pit. Fathers and mothers and children. The mothers had to watch the way they killed their children. In one moment, the past perished with the future. The blood of parents and children, bridegrooms and brides mixed together – a mixture of blood in one pit.

V'yibchu Bnei Yisrael et haserefa asher saraf Hashem – the Children of Israel should cry over the fire which Hashem burnt. Where does one get the words to express such a *churban*? From where does one get the tears to mourn all of the thousands who perished in the *Grosse Aktion?* Where can one find the tears to cry for those who fell in all of the *Aktionen* – not just that of Kovno, but of all of the cities and villages of Lithuania; of the precious Jews who perished *al kiddush Hashem* – in sanctification of God's Name? It is a tragedy that has never been equaled.

"V'yibchu Bnei Yisrael et haserefa asher saraf Hashem. I wish to write just like *Yirmeyahu* mourning over Jerusalem, "*Eichah yashevah badad ha-ir?* – How deserted lies the city?"[343] – How is it that Kovno remains isolated, without Jews? How is it that all the cities and villages in Lithuania are left without Jews? Our Sages say that God mourned over Adam, the first man, with the word "*Eichah* – How?"[344] From where do I know this? Because it says in the verse, "*Va-yomer lo ayyekkah* – And He said to him, 'Where are you?'[345]." In Hebrew, *ayyekkah* – where – is spelled with the same letters as *eichah* – how.[346]

"I also would like to express *eichah* with the word *ayyekkah.*[347] Where are you, Kovno Jews? Where are you, Kovno-Slobodka Yeshivah with your precious yeshivah *bachurim*? Where are you, Kovno synagogues, in which people prayed by day and by night? Where are you, Jewish gymnasia – Yavneh Gymnasium, Ral Gymnasium, Shvabes Gymnasium? Where are you, Jewish youth of Lithuania? Where are you, all the Jews of the cities and villages of Lithuania? *Ayyekkah?*

"They did not allow you to rest in graves. After two years lying in the graves, they uncovered you and incinerated you so that no *zecher* [memory] of you would remain.[348] *Yirmeyahu*, the prophet, says, "*Ki gadol ka'yam shivrech* – Your disaster is as large as the sea."[349] Why does the prophet say "*Ka'yam*" – like the sea – and not "*Ka'aretz*" – like the land? Is the land not large enough? Rather, when a catastrophe occurs on land, one can see its remains thousands of years later. I was once in Naples, Italy, and I searched for the obliterated city of Pompeii, which was destroyed by a volcano. One can still see, to this day, the ashes. One can see the petrified, half-burned people – horror. Yet, when a disaster takes place at sea, such as when a ship sinks – such a disaster can only be seen at the moment the ship goes under. After a while, the water covers it, and the sea is as beautiful, as if nothing had happened.

"That is what the prophet means when he states, *Ki gadol kayam shivrech* – that after the *churban*, professors and colleges will come and say that the Holocaust never happened; they will deny the Holocaust. We, the living *matzevot* [gravestones] and the State of Israel after us, will not allow [the world] to deny the Holocaust.

"Thank G-d, we, the *she'erith hapleitah*, we, the *atzamot ha'yeveshot* [dry bones], we, the *udim mutzalim me'esh* [brands plucked out of the fire] – we have established beautiful families, we have lived to see the building up of the Land of Israel; and we can say that *Am Yisrael chai* – the Jewish people live and will live *le'olam va'ed* – forever and ever."[350]

> G-d, full of mercy, Who dwells on high, grant proper rest on the wings of the Divine Presence, in the exalted levels of the holy and the pure, who shine like the brilliance of the firmament – for the holy souls that were killed, slaughtered, burned, drowned, and hanged for the sanctification of G-d's Name, at the time of the *Shoah* in Lithuania, by the hands of the Nazis, may their names be erased. Perform this for the sake of the congregation, who will donate charity in remembrance of their souls. May their resting place be in the Garden of Eden. Therefore, may the Master of Mercy bring them close to the shelter of His wings for eternity; and may He bind their souls in the Bond of Life. Hashem is their heritage and may they lie in peace on their resting place. Now let us respond: Amen.

(Left to Right): Yitzhak Meir Schames holding his son Dov Schames, Leib Schames standing center, Chiene Schames holding her daughter Rochel Devorah Schames.
Kovno, Lithuania, circa 1925

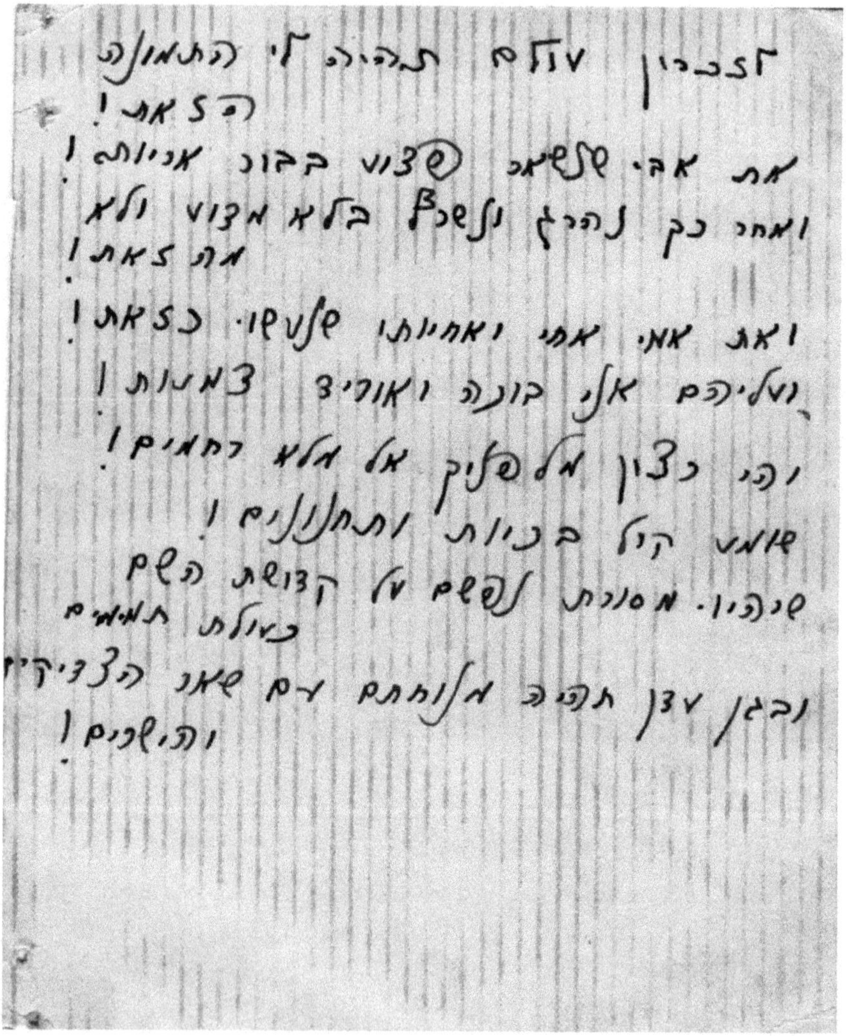

This poem was written by Leib on the back of the family photo shown on the previous page.

Translation:

This photo should serve as an eternal memorial to me!

My father, who was left wounded in the lion's den!

And, afterwards he was murdered and burned without reason or purpose!

And, my mother, brother and sister who were done the same!

And, on them I cry and shed tears!

May it be Your will, G-d, filled with mercy!

Who listens to the sounds of cries and supplication!

That they who passed their souls in sanctification of God's Name be like a perfect offering!

And may they rest in the Garden of Eden with the rest of the righteous and the straight!

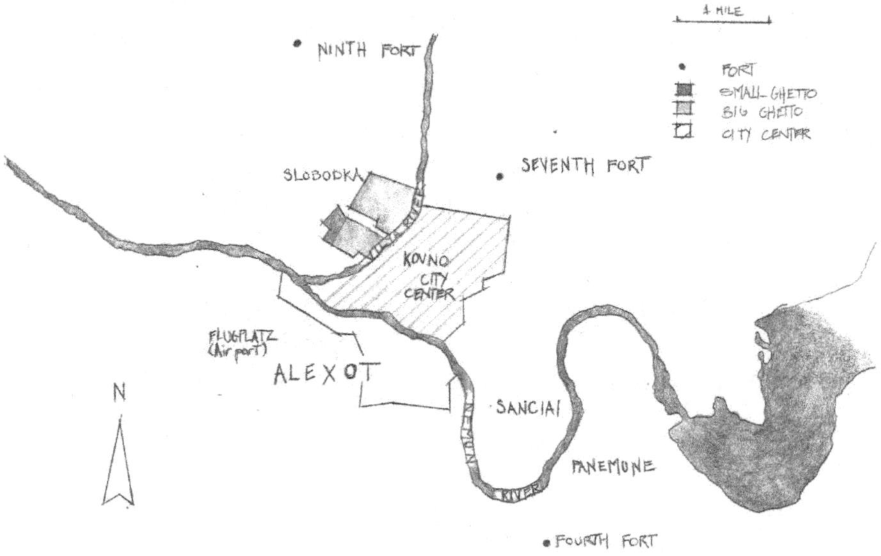

City of Kovno

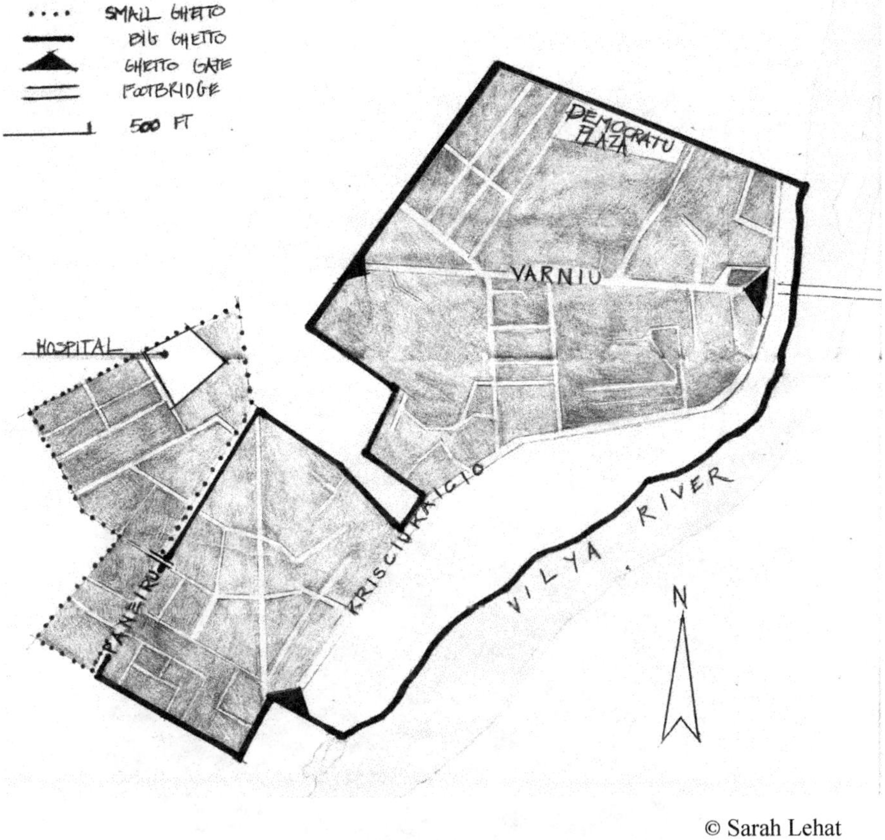

© Sarah Lehat

Map of the Kovno Ghetto

The Ninth Fort

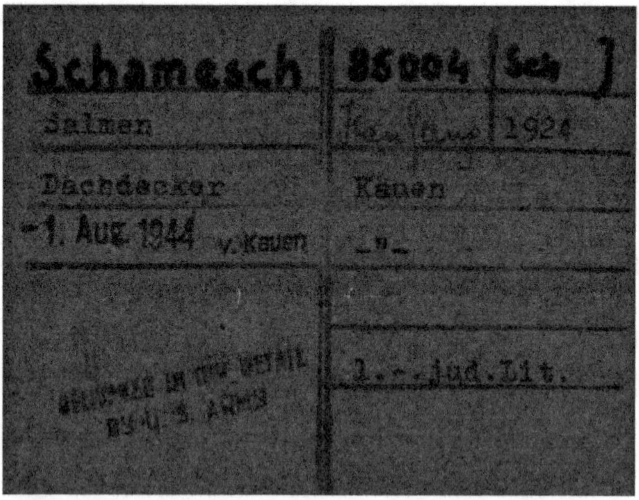

Schamesch | 85004 | Sch

Salmen | 1924

Dachdecker | Kauen

1. Aug. 1944 v. Kauen | -"-

1.-- Jud. Lit.

Leib's Kaufering Registration Card. He is referred to by his legal name, Zalman (spelled here Salmen).

[Courtesy of International Tracing Service (ITS), Germany]

(Left to Right) Leib and unidentified friend
Germany, circa 1945

Leib Schames
Bailly, France circa 1946

(Left to Right): Leib Schames, Chana Nodel (nee Izikovitz), Devorah Bella Izikovitz, Yitzhak Izikovitz

France, circa 1947

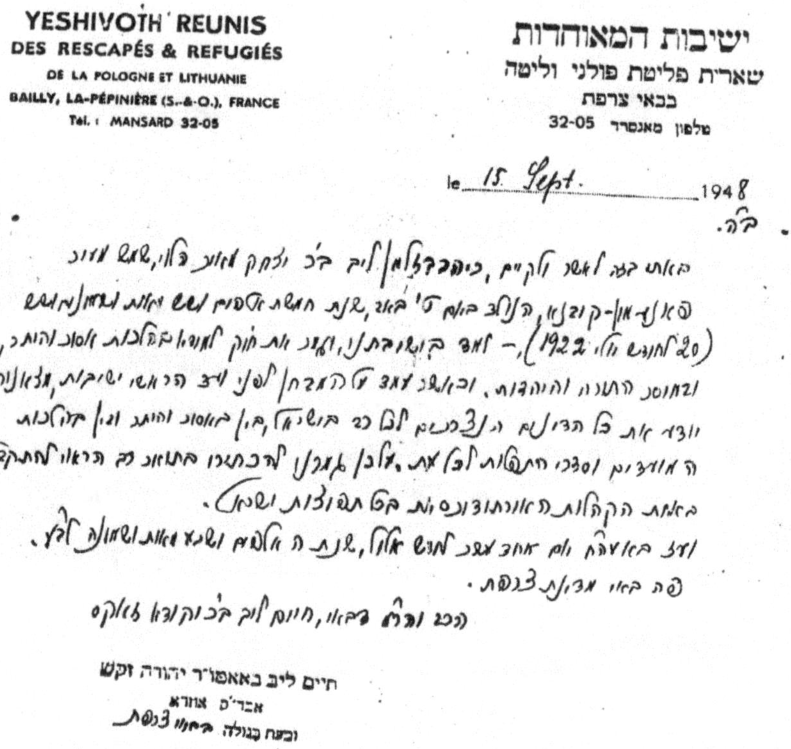

YESHIVOTH REUNIS
DES RESCAPÉS & REFUGIÉS
DE LA POLOGNE ET LITHUANIE
BAILLY, LA-PÉPINIÈRE (S.-&-O.), FRANCE
Tél. : MANSARD 32-05

ישיבות המאוחדות
שארית פליטת פולני וליטה
בבאי צרפת
טלפון מאנסרד 32-05

le 15 Sept. 1948

ב"ה

חיים ליב באאפו"ר יהודה זקש
אבד"ק אוורא
וכעת בגולה בבאיי צרפת

Leib's Rabbinic Ordination from the yeshivah in Bailly, signed by Rabbi Chaim Leib Zacks.

Bailly, France September 15, 1948

Wedding of Esther Izikovitz and Leib Schames
Cleveland, 1952

Leib and Esther at their wedding

(Left to Right, front row): Esther Izikovitz, Leib Schames, unidentified child, Rabbi Eliyahu-Meir Bloch, their *mesader kiddushin.* Cleveland, 1952

Esther and Leib
Los Angeles, circa 1990

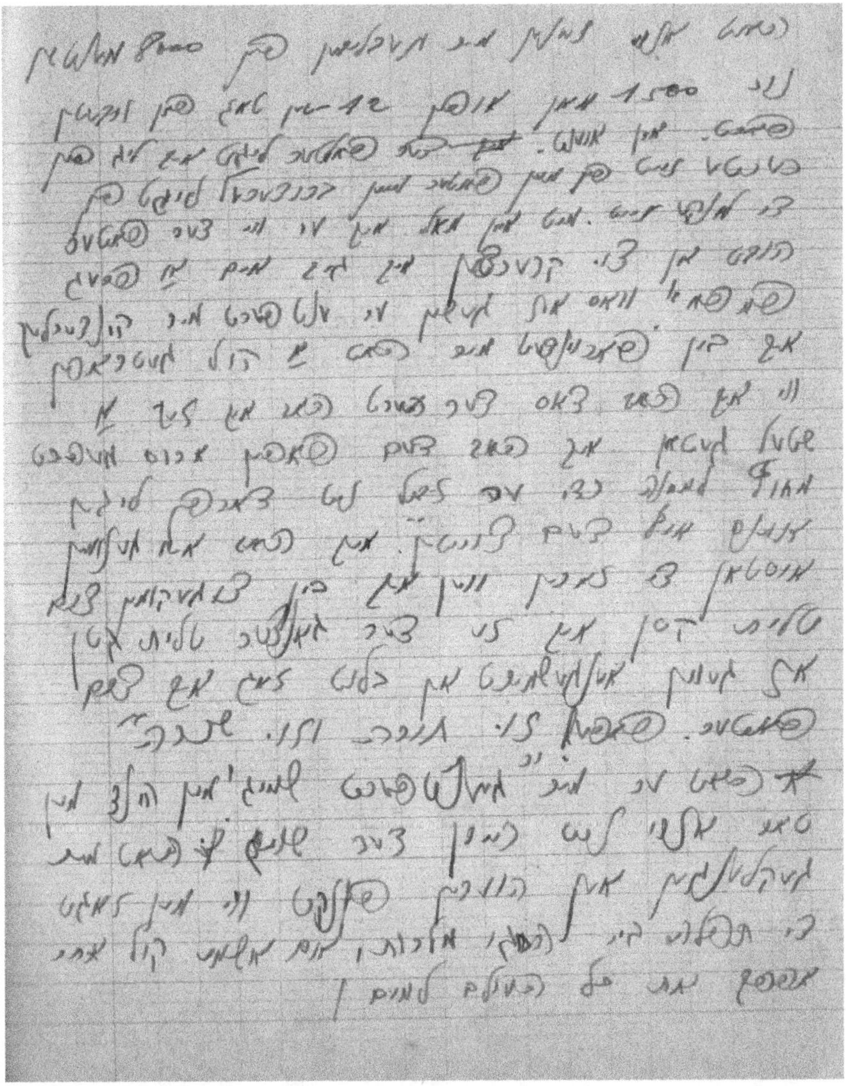

A page of Leib's memoir, written in Yiddish, June 19, 1947; the page describes Leib and his father in the Seventh Fort (translation found on pages 36-37).

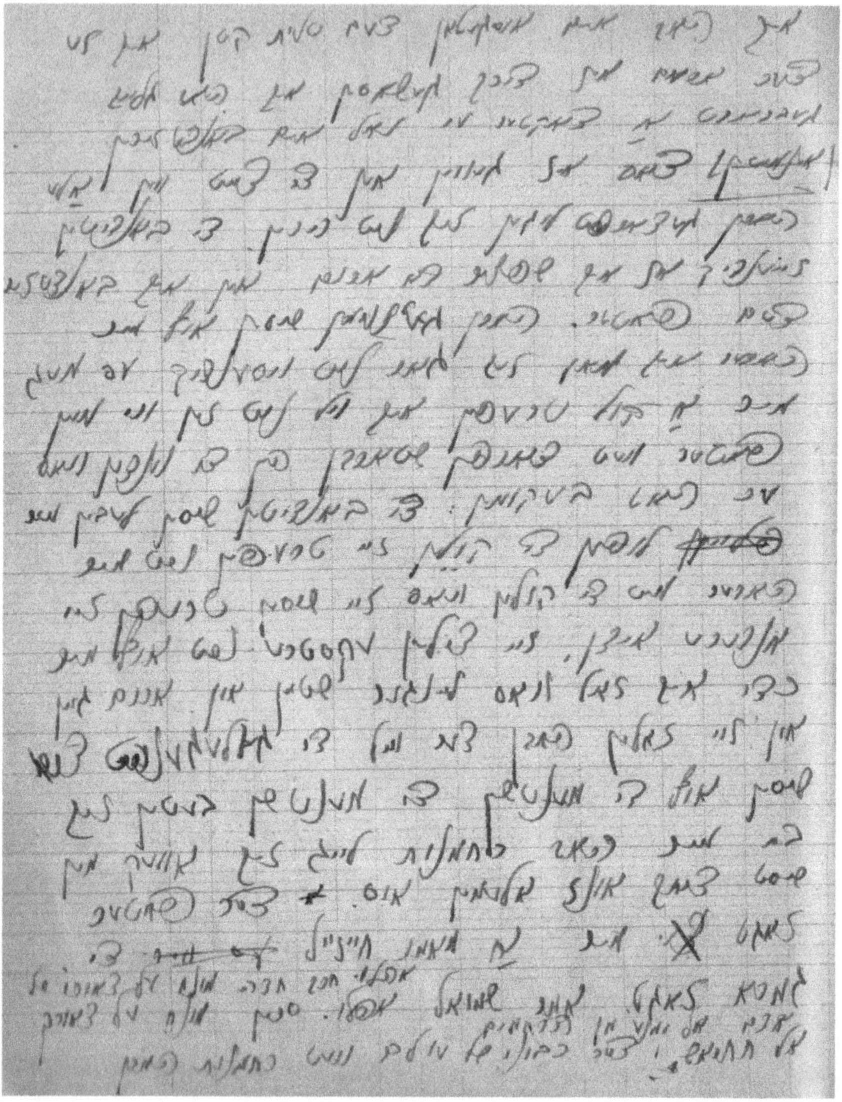

The next page of Leib's memoir, written in Yiddish, June 19, 1947; the page describes the last conversation between Leib and his father before his father's death (translation found on pages 36-37).

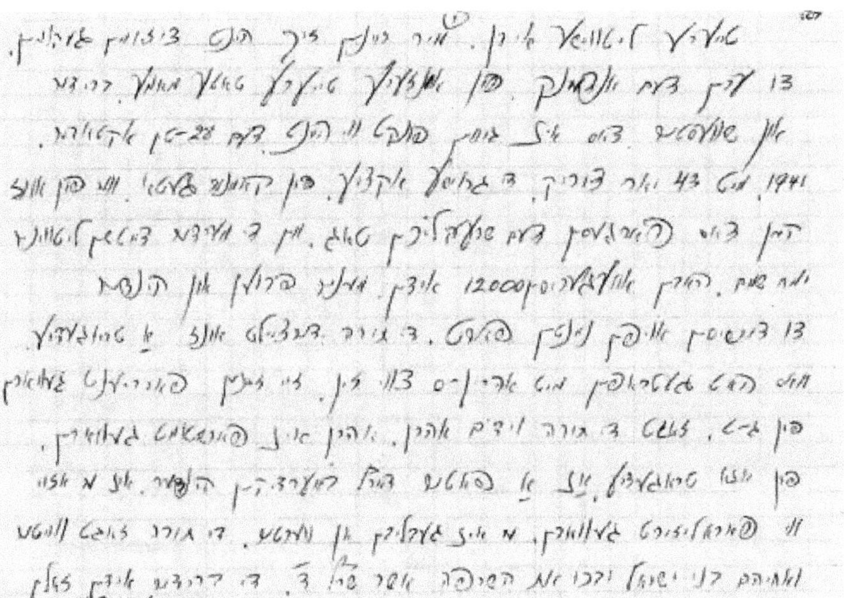

Leib's 1984 speech, "Dear Lithuanian Jews", page 1

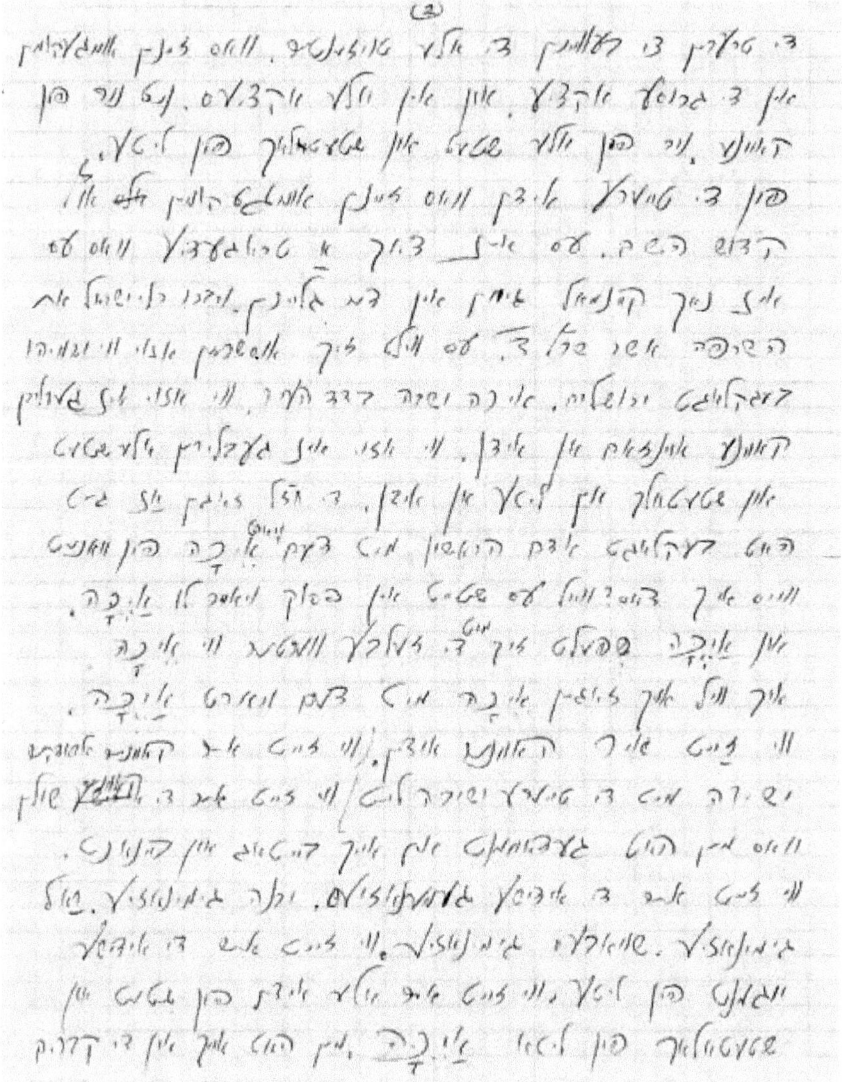

Leib's 1984 speech, "Dear Lithuanian Jews", page 2

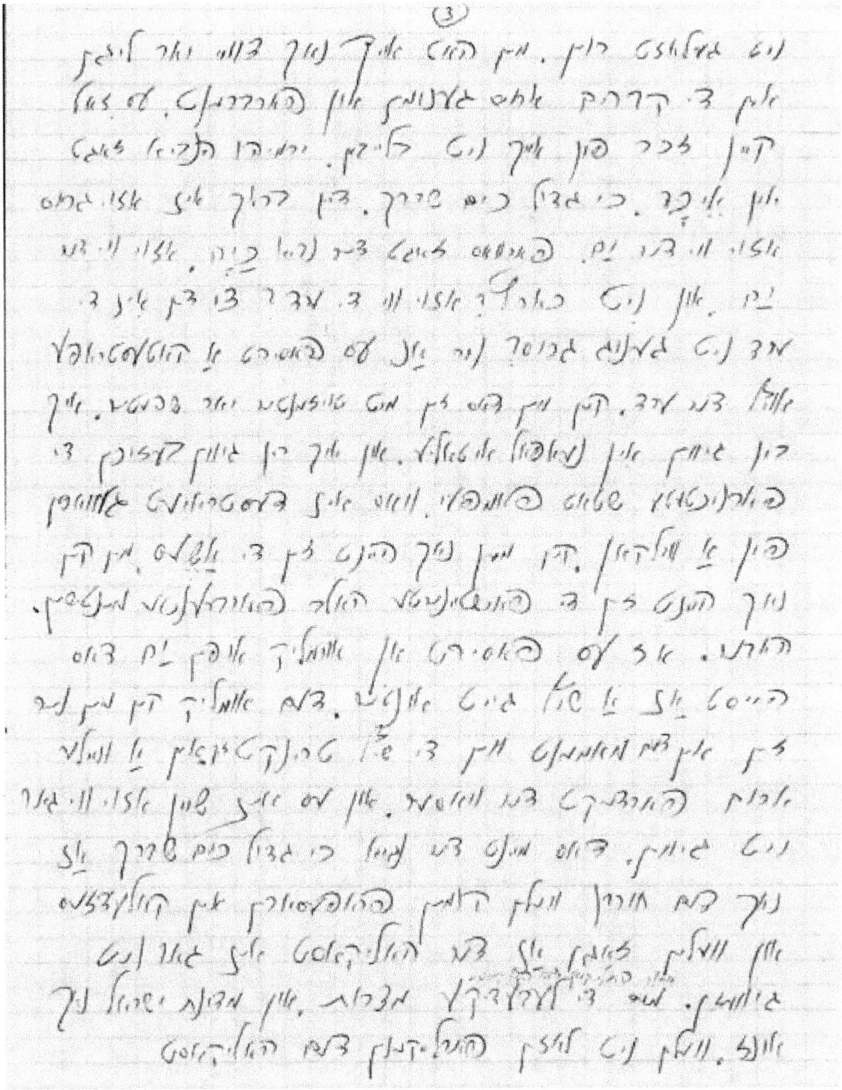

Leib's 1984 speech, "Dear Lithuanian Jews", page 3

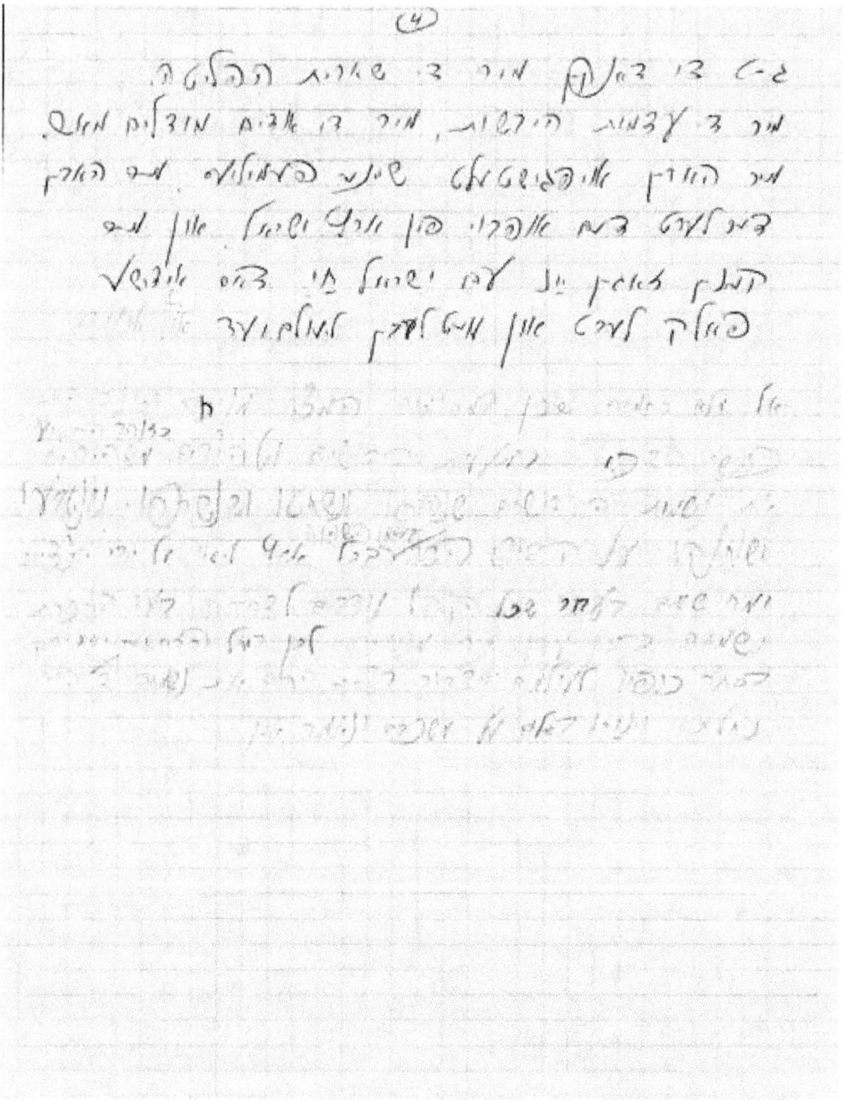

Leib's 1984 speech, "Dear Lithuanian Jews", page 4

Glossary

Adam, the first man: The first man, described in the Bible in Genesis 1:26-31, 2:7-25 and 3:1-23.

Aktion (pl. Aktionen): German term used to describe roundups, pogroms, and usually, mass murder.

Al kiddush Hashem: Lit., "In sanctification of G-d's Name." Usually associated with loosing one's life for his or her religion. Though it is used in this context throughout the book, it can also be used to mean actions which create a positive image for G-d and the Jewish people.

Almighty: Another Name for G-d.

Alav hashalom: Term used for a person who has passed away. In English parlance it means may he or she rest in peace.

Aliyah: Lit.,"go up." This is a common phrase used by Jews to mean immigration to the Land of Israel.

Am Yisrael chai: Lit., "The Nation of Israel lives." An affirmation that despite suffering and mass murder, the Jewish people will always live.

Amalek: Eternal enemy of the Jewish people, infamous for attacking the Jewish people in the beginning of their sojourning in the desert (See Deuteronomy 25:17-19). Throughout Jewish history, any enemy of the Jewish people, especially one that attempts to murder Jews, can be referred to as *Amalek.*

Anuyim kashim: Lit., "harsh afflictions."

Appellplatz: Yard in the camp where roll call takes place.

Atzamot ha'yeveshot: Lit., "Dry bones." According to a literal reading of Ezekiel 37:2, *atzamot ha'yeveshot* refers to the prophecy where despite resignation and insurmountable obstacles, G-d will save the Jewish people and bring them to the Land of Israel (See Ezekiel 37:2).

Av: Eleventh month in the Jewish year. This month is usually defined by sadness as this was the month when the two Jewish Temples were destroyed.

Baba Metzia: Tractate in the Talmud dealing mostly with civil laws.

Bachurim: Young, unmarried students in a yeshivah.

Balak: Seventh *Parashah* in the book of Numbers. The *Parashah* is named after Balak, the King of Moav. After seeing how G-d aided the Jews in war, he hired the gentile prophet, Bilam, to curse the Jews (See Numbers 22:2-6).

Bar Mitzvah: A coming of age ritual where boys who reached the age of thirteen become bound to perform *mitzvot*. Traditionally, the boy reads the *parashah* for the week when he turns thirteen.

Beitar: Revisionist Zionist youth group founded by Ze'ev Jabotinsky in 1923. This nationalistic group believed in training Jews militarily to fight all forms of anti-Semitism and to control the Land of Israel.

Beit midrash (pl. beitei midrashim): Lit., "Houses of Study". Place where Jews gather to study the Torah.

Berachos: Lit. "blessings." Can be referring to any blessing or the first tractate in the Talmud dealing with the laws of blessings and prayers.

Big Ghetto: See small ghetto.

Bnei Yisrael: Lit., "The Children of Israel." The term is used synonymously with Jews.

Bereishis: Lit., "In the beginning" or "Genesis;" first *Parashah* in the Pentateuch. It is also the name given to the first book of five in the Pentateuch, commonly referred to as Genesis.

Brigades: Jewish labor groups in the ghetto operating in various industries within Kovno.

Capo: Prisoners, made up of both Jews and gentiles alike, who were appointed the head of a labor squad in a concentration camp. They retained privileges advantageous to survival compared to their subordinates.

Chazal: Lit., "our Sages." Refers to Rabbis of the Talmud and sometimes later authorities.

Cheder or Heder: Lit., "room." A school for young children, usually held in the teacher's home where elementary studies like Hebrew grammar and Bible were taught.

Chizuk: Lit., "strengthening."

Commandant: Chief commanding officer.

Chulin: Tractate dealing with the *halakha* of kosher food.

Churban: Lit., "destruction;" Often used synonymously with the Holocaust.

Eglah arupha: An animal sacrifice that must be slaughtered if a murdered corpse is found in a field between two cities and the court does not know the identity of the perpetrator.

Eichah: Also known as Lamentations, *Eichah* describes the destruction of the First Temple and is commonly read on *Tisha B'Av*. See *Tisha B'Av*.

Em ha'banim semecha: Lit., "A glad mother of children;" quote from Psalm 113 describing how G-d will uplift those suffering and destitute. The context of the verse reads, "He transforms the barren wife, into a glad mother of children, Hallelluyah."

Eretz Yisrael: Lit., "Land of Israel." Referred to as the "Promise Land," the "Holy Land," or the "Land of Canaan." Throughout their history Jews have longed to immigrate and return to the Land of Israel.

The Fourth Fort: One of Nine Forts surrounding Kovno. Built along with the First through the Eight Fort in the nineteenth century, the Fort served to protect Kovno (then under Russian control) from Germany and Poland. On August 7th and August 18th, 1941, Lithuanian fascists murdered about fifteen hundred Jews there.

Flugplatz: German military airport located in the Kovno suburb of Alexot. The main site for slave labor in the Kovno ghetto; thousands of Jews worked at the *Flugplatz* to build a runway.

Garden of Eden: Known as paradise, the place where Adam and Eve lived before their exile. It can also mean heaven.

Gemara: Commentary on the Mishnah recording the arguments of the Rabbis, Jewish Law, stories, and parables. See Talmud.

Gestapo: The Nazi secret police force.

Grace after Meals: Benediction said after partaking of bread.

The Grosse Aktion: Lit., "The Big *Aktion*" or "The Great *Aktion*."

Gymnasium: Lithuanian schools where secular subjects were taught in addition to Torah.

Habad: See Lubavitch.

Halakha: Jewish law.

Harugei malchut: Ten martyred Sages murdered by the Roman government. Their deaths are commemorated most prominently in the *Yom Kippur Mussaf* prayer, *Eleh Ezkerah*.

Haggadah: Lit., "telling." This refers to the book read on the first (and second night of Passover in the Diaspora), on what is known popularly as the *Seder* night. The book contains rituals, songs, reflections, and insights into the story of the Exodus. The leader of the *Seder* uses the *Haggadah* as a platform to question and stimulate his audience's (specifically children's) attention and thought.

Hashem: Lit., "The Name." Term used to refer to G-d.

Hasid: Lit., "pious one." A follower of the movement founded by Rabbi Israel ben Eliezer, Baal Shem Tov (circa 1700-1760) and his students. *Hasidim* (pl. *Hasid*) often stressed the importance of prayer, conscious devotion, and closeness to G-d. *Hasidim* usually follow a "Rebbe" or "*tzaddik*" whose deeds they admire and whose dictates they adhere. *Hasidim* have often been contrasted with the *misnagdim* (lit., those who "oppose" the *Hasidim*) who are seen as less emotional and more concerned with Talmud study than prayer.

Haskalah: The Jewish enlightenment. In Eastern Europe, the movement leaders (known as *maskilim*) aimed to modernize Judaism and enact moderate reform. The early *maskilim* were more conservative in their aims.

Jauna Lietuva: Lit., "Young Lithuanians." A fascist-Lithuanian group for young people modeled on Nazi ideology whose members would later murder hundreds of Jews. Prior to the Holocaust, the group had about forty thousand members.

The Jewish Police: Operating under the *Judenrat*, the Jewish ghetto police controlled crime and carried out *Judenrat* and German orders. The entire history of the Jewish ghetto police in Kovno remains complex. The Jewish police should not be viewed as entirely cooperative with the German authorities. There were some policemen who sadistically complied with Nazi orders and extortioned funds from smugglers. Others played a more nuanced role, assisting everyday Jews when they had the opportunity and acting valiantly on the community's behalf.

Joint Distribution Committee: American charitable fund providing support and financial assistance to survivors in Europe.

Jordan passes: Named after German Commander of Ghetto Affairs in Kovno, Sturmfuehrer Jordan, these passes indicated which Jews were of working status. They were believed by many in the ghetto to be "life passes" that could be used to escape *Aktions*.

Judenrat: The Jewish governing body in the ghetto.

Kabbalah: The esoteric and mystical teachings of Judaism.

Kaufering: A group of eleven subsidiary camps of the Dachau Concentration Camp. Most prisoners at Kaufering worked as slave laborers building underground bases for German forces.

Kiddushin: Tractate in the Talmud which describe the laws of marriage.

Kinder Aktion: Lit., "The Children's *Aktion.*"

Kittel: White robe worn by Jewish men at solemn occasions such as weddings, the Passover *Seder*, and *Yom Kippur.*

Knesset Yisrael Yeshivah or Slobodka Yeshivah: Famous *mussar* yeshivah located in the small suburb of Slobodka. The Yeshivah attracted students from around the world. *Knesset Yisrael* had a prefatory school called *Ohel Moshe* and *Ohr Yisrael.* All of these institutions would ultimately be known as the Slobodka Yeshivah. *Knesset Yisrael* (lit., "Congregation of Israel") is named after Rabbi Yisrael Salanter, evoking ties to his *mussar* movement. See *mussar* and Rabbi Yisrael Salanter.

Koach: Lit., "power" or "strength."

Labor Office: A Jewish government body under the Judenrat managing the labor force in the Kovno Ghetto.

Lithuanian fascists: Also referred to here as "Lithuanian bandits" or "bandits." Lithuanian fascists refers to ultranationalist Lithuanian gentiles who held ideas similar to Nazism. The Lithuanian fascists murdered many Jews immediately after the Germans invasion of Kovno and assisted the Germans during the ghetto period.

Litvaks: Syn., "Lithuanian Jews." Those Jews who lived in Lithuania which included parts of Eastern Poland, Western Russian, Belarus and Latvia.

Lubavitch Hasid: Also known as *Habad.* A type of *Hasidic* group, one of the few *Hasidic* groups with a large population residing in Lithuania, founded by the Rabbi Shnuer Zalman of Liadi.

Maariv: Prayer service held at night. One of the three services religious Jews say daily.

Mamrei Chazal: Lit., "Saying from our Sages"

Mashgiach: Spiritual Head of a yeshivah. Unlike the *Rosh Yeshivah* who usually gives lectures in Talmud, the *Mashgiach* is often in charge of providing spiritual guidance and developing student talents and character.

Matzevot: Lit., "gravestones."

Messechet: Lit., "Tractate."

Menachos: Tractate in the Talmud dealing with offerings as well as other laws including *tzitzis.*

Mesader Kiddushin: Officiator of a Jewish marriage ceremony.

Mitzvah (pl. Mitzvot): Lit., "commandments." According to Jewish tradition, there are six hundred and thirteen *mitzvot* in the Torah, three hundred and sixty-five negative ones and two hundred and forty-eight positive ones.

Moll: Short for the Leohnard Moll construction firm. The company contracted with the German government to build a bombproof hidden base, concealed from aerial view, to store an arsenal of fighter planes. The administrators at the construction firm bought Kaufering inmates daily to work at a construction site near Kaufering.

Mussar: Nineteenth and twentieth century ethical movement, promoted by Rabbi Yisrael Salanter. Teachers of the movement emphasized conscious devotion to G-d and self examination in order to improve character traits. The Slobodka Yeshivah was known as a *mussar* yeshivah, a school which emphasized *mussar* teachings and the study of religious ethical works such as *Chovot Halevavot* [Duties of the Heart] in addition to intensive study of the Talmud. A follower of this movement can be called a *Mussarist* or *Mussarnik.*

Musselman (*pl. Musselmanner*): Emaciated and starving inmates in the camps.

Nazi Motorized Transport Corp or N.S.K.K.: A motor organization who, at points in time, operated as guards within the Kovno ghetto.

The Ninth Fort: One of Nine Forts which surrounded the city of Kovno. Though built in the early twentieth century to defend Lithuania (then Russia) from its enemies, the Ninth fort later served as a Russian prison. After the German army captured Kovno in June 1941, the site was used as the main execution site for the Jewish population in Kovno.

Nissan: Seventh month in the Jewish year. The month usually falls around March and April. The Jews left Egypt during this month and therefore Passover takes place during this month.

Nekamah: Lit., "Revenge."

Nes: Lit,. "miracle."

Operation Barbarossa: Code name for Nazi Germany's invasion of the Soviet Union, which began June 22, 1941.

Olam Habah: Lit., "the world to come." In modern parlance, this is heaven.

Parshat or Parshah: A section of the Pentateuch read weekly on the Sabbath. A different *Parashah* is read every Sabbath and the Pentateuch is thus completed yearly.

Parshat Ha'Shavua: Weekly *Parshah* read every Shabbat. See *Parshat.*

Passuk: Lit., "verse." Verse in a sacred text.

Pesach or Passover: The holiday commemorating the Exodus from Egypt. See *Haggadah.*

Peshat: The simple, sometimes superficial interpretation, of the text.

Purim: A holiday celebrating the salvation from the wicked Haman and his plot to destroy the Jews of Ancient Persia. The story of Purim is recorded in the book of Esther.

Red Army: The Russian-Communist army.

Rosh Hashanah: Lit., "The Head of the Year." The Jewish New Year, a time for feasts, introspection, and prayer, when Jews ask G-d for a successful and healthy new year. This is also the name of a tractate in the Talmud.

Rosh Yeshivah: Rector of a yeshivah. Provides advanced lectures in Talmud. See *Mashgiach.*

Sauguma: The Lithuanian Police.

Shecht: Lit., "slaughter."

Sefer Torah (pl. sifrei torah): Torah scroll usually housed in the ark at the eastern front of a synagogue.

Sefer (pl. seforim): Lit., "book." Usually refers to any sacred book.

The Seventh Fort: One of Nine Forts surrounding Kovno. Built along with the First through the Eighth Fort in the nineteenth century to protect Kovno (then under Russian control) from Germany and Poland. During the early part of the German occupation of Lithuania, Lithuanian and German fascists murdered thousands of Jews there.

Shabbat: The "Day of Rest" where religious Jews stop their work duties from early Friday evening until Saturday night. This is usually a time of great joy in a Jewish household where families eat festive meals together and attend synagogue.

Shavuot: Lit., "Weeks." It is also known as the Holiday of *Bikkurim* as Jews would travel to Jerusalem to bring *Bikkurim* – the seven fruits – for which the Land of Israel is praised. These include wheat, barley, grapes, figs, pomegranates, olives, and dates. The holiday also commemorates the anniversary for G-d's giving of the Torah at Mount Sinai. The book of Ruth is customarily read during this holiday.

Shelach: Fourth *Parashah* in the book of Numbers.

Shema or Shema Yisrael Adonai Eloheinu Adonai Echad: Lit., Hear O' Israel Hashem is our G-d, Hashem is One. Cardinal prayer in Judaism, affirming G-d's Oneness, which religious Jews state three times daily. The prayer is additionally said before a Jew is about to die.

Shoah: Lit., "The catastrophe." This term is used primarily by Hebrew speaking Jews to describe the genocide of European Jewry between 1941-1945. It is synonymous with the English term, Holocaust.

Shtender: Elevated, small desk for individuals to place their books during Torah study.

Schochet: Person who slaughters kosher animals according to *halakha.*

Shofar: Ram horn traditionally blown on *Rosh Hashanah* to symbolically coronate G-d as the Master of the Universe.

She'erith Hapleitah: Lit., "The Leftover Remnant." This term was coined by survivors, after the Holocaust, to connote the few who remained alive after the Nazi genocide.

Siddur: Jewish prayer book.

Simchat Torah: Holiday immediately following *Sukkot* where Jews celebrate the completion and the beginning of the Pentateuch. This was considered a major holiday in Lithuania as Jews rejoiced with *sifrei* Torahs and exuberantly danced in the synagogue.

Sivan: Ninth month according to the Hebrew calendar.

The Sixth Fort: One of Nine Forts surrounding Kovno. Built along with the First through the Eighth Fort in the late nineteenth century, the Fort served to protect Kovno (then under Russian control) from its enemies. During the Holocaust, the Fort served as an execution site during the early part of the German occupation.

Slobodka: Old suburb in Kovno. Heavily populated Jewish, often religious, area. The *Knesset Yisrael* Yeshivah stood in Slobodka. The suburb contained dilapidated buildings, facilities and homes. During the Holocaust, the Kovno Ghetto stood in this area.

Slobodka Yeshivah: See *Knesset Yisrael.*

Small Ghetto: The Small Ghetto was a small area in the Kovno Ghetto. At the time of the Kovno Ghetto's creation, some two thousand and five hundred Jews lived in the Small Ghetto, compared with twenty-seven thousand and five hundred in the other area, the Big Ghetto. On October 4, 1941, the Germans and Lithuanian destroyed the Small Ghetto and murdered some two thousand Jews there. The surviving Jews of the Small Ghetto moved into the Big Ghetto.

S.S. or Schulzstaffel: Lit., "Protection Squadron." Principle agency for surveillance and mass murder in German occupied land.

Sugya. (pl. sugyot): Section in the Talmud.

Sukkot: Holiday of booths where Jews sit in small man-made huts to commemorate G-d's protection during the Jewish people's sojourn in the desert.

Sukkah or succahs: Lit., "booths." See *Sukkot.*

Tallis katan: A four cornered garment with four strings attached to each corner. It is customarily worn by men under their shirt. Another name for a *tallis katan* is *tzitzis.*

Talmud: The Talmud is composed of the *Mishnah* and the *Gemara*, a commentary on the *Mishnah*. The Talmud is the central text which records the arguments of the Rabbis, *halakha*, stories and parables.

Tammuz: Tenth Month in the Hebrew Calendar.

Techelet: A blue dye used to color one (or two) of the four strings on each corner of the *tallis katan*.

Tefillin: Two black shaped boxes containing parchment with verses written from the Torah. *Tefillin* are customarily worn by men during morning prayers, serving as a reminder of the Exodus and to focus one's time for spiritual growth.

Telz Yeshivah: Famous yeshivah founded in 1875 in the city of Telz. The yeshivah operated until the Holocaust when the Nazis and their Lithuanian collaborators savagely murdered the Jewish community of Telz. Founded by Rabbis from the original Lithuanian Yeshivah, a Telz Yeshivah operated in Cleveland, Ohio from World War II onwards.

Three Weeks: A three week period of mourning commemorating the beginning of the destruction of the Temple which culminates on *Tisha B'Av*. The period starts from the Seventeenth of *Tammuz* until the Ninth of *Av*. As a sign of mourning, religious Jews do not get haircuts or listen to music during this time.

Throne of Glory: The term is mentioned in the books of the Prophets (see i.e., Kings I 22:19). A mystical term described allegorically by Maimonides in his *Guide for the Perplexed*.

Tisha B'Av: Lit., "The Ninth of [the month of] *Av*." A day of mourning commemorating the destruction of the Jewish Temples.

Tishrei: First month in the Jewish year, usually taking place during the months of September or October. Many holidays are celebrated in *Tishrei* including *Rosh Hashanah*, *Yom Kippur* and *Sukkot*.

Torah: Though often synonymous with the Pentateuch, the Torah usually encompasses all holy writings, from the *Prophets* to the *Midrash* to the *Gemara*, even commentary written today.

Tzaddik: A righteous individual.

Tzitzis: See *tallis katan*.

Udim mutzalim me'esh: Lit., "Brands plucked from the fire." See Zechariah 3:2.

Vayikra: Third book in the Pentateuch and the name of the first *Parshah* in this book.

Vidui: Verbal confessions part and parcel of the repentance process. *Vidui* is also customarily said before one is expected to die.

Wehrmacht: Nazi-German armed forces.

Yahrzeit: The anniversary of an individual's death.

Yatom: Lit., "An orphan."

Yamim Noraim: Lit., "Days of Awe." Usually refers to the time from *Rosh Hashanah* until *Yom Kippur*. During this time, Jews ask forgiveness from G-d for the prior year's sins and pray, ideally with a sense of awe and trepidation, for a year of success and health for the upcoming year.

Yemach shemam: Lit., "may their names be erased."

Yeshivah (pl. Yeshivot): Religious secondary school where male students spend most of their day studying the Talmud. In pre-Holocaust Lithuania, the *Knesset Yisrael* yeshivah (also known as the Slobodka Yeshivah, as the yeshivah building stood in the suburb of Slobodka) was one of the most famous yeshivot in the entire world.

Yeshivah Gedolah: Yeshivah for advanced teenagers and young adults.

Yeshivah Ketanah: Yeshivah for younger children and teenagers, usually between the ages of twelve and eighteen.

Yirmeyahu (or Jeremiah): Hebrew prophet and author of the book of *Eichah* or Lamentations. *Eichah* describes the destruction of the First Temple and is commonly read on *Tisha B'Av*, the day which commemorates the destructions of the Temple. The book *Yirmeyahu* is named after this prophet.

Yom Tov: Lit., "A good day." A holiday devoted to the learning of sacred texts, prayer and rejoicing with food and drink. Certain labors are forbidden during this time except for cooking and carrying. Examples of *Yom Tov* are *Rosh Hashanah* and the first two days of *Sukkot* and Passover.

Yushnik: A soup made up of horse meat and water provided by the Germans to Jews in the Kovno ghetto.

Zecher: Lit.,"memory."

Zionism: Nineteenth and twentieth century Jewish national-political movement whose adherents advocated emigration to the Land of Israel.

zt"l: Acronym for *Zecher Tzaddik L'brachah* – the remembrance of a righteous individual brings blessing.

Glossary of Names

Chiene Schames (circa 1902-1941). Leib's mother. She was ultimately murdered, along with six of her seven children, at the Ninth Fort, on the eighth of *Cheshvan* (October 29, 1941).

Dov Schames (circa 1924-1941). Leib's younger brother and twin brother of Rochel Schames. He was murdered on the eighth of *Cheshvan* (October 29, 1941) along with his mother and siblings.

Elijah. Prophet during the Ninth Century BCE known for his zeal in the service of G-d. Regarded as the harbinger of the Messiah, he is mentioned throughout Jewish ritual, including the Passover *Seder*.

Elijah ben Solomon (1720-1797). See Gaon of Vilna.

Elisha ben Avuyah. Religious authority who lived after the destruction of the Second Temple, around 70 CE. He is the teacher of Rabbi Meir. After seeing, according to one tradition, the tongue of a Torah scholar dragged through the streets by a pig, he exclaimed, "The mouth that uttered pearls of Torah now licks the dust," and became a heretic. According to the Talmud (Babli, Chagigah 15b; Yerushalmi, Chagigah 77b), he repented at the end of his life and entered heaven.

Gaon of Vilna, Vilna Gaon, or **GRA**. Popular name for Rabbi Elijah ben Solomon (1720-1797), the greatest scholar in Lithuania. Rabbi Elijah was known for his rare genius, asceticism, and piety. He was regarded as the leader of all Lithuania Jewry.

Helmut Rauca (1908-1983). German commandant of Gestapo Security and infamous administrator of the *Grosse Aktion*. He later emigrated to Canada, where due to the great inefficiency and indifference on the part of the Canadian government, he was not tried until 1982, some forty one years after the *Grosse Aktion*. He was eventually extradited to Germany where he died of cancer before his trial.

Judith Meisel (1929-present). Member of Leib's smuggling group, lead by Motke. Survivor of the Kovno Ghetto and Stutthof.

Molotov or **Vyacheslav Molotov** (1890-1986). Soviet politician and diplomat.

Motke (circa 1920 – circa 1948). Manager of Leib's smuggling group and lead trader. One of the heads of the black market in the Kovno ghetto.

Moshe Levine (?-1944). Commander of the Jewish ghetto police. Member of the Zionist underground in the ghetto. Levine was ultimately murdered in the Ninth Fort on the day of the *Kinder Aktion* for refusing to provide information about hiding places in the ghetto.

Nathan Kodikow [also spelled Codikov] (1923-1941). Best friend of Leib and resident of Panemune. Ultimately murdered in the Seventh Fort.

Nicholas of Russia or **Nicholas II** (1868-1918). Last Emperor of Russia.

Rabbi Akiva (circa 40 CE – circa 137 CE). A leading Sage quoted in the *Mishnah*. Thousands of students studied under him. He was later murdered by the Roman government in the aftermath of the Bar Kokhba revolt.

Rabbi Avraham Grodzinski (1883-1944). *Mashgiach* of Knesset Yisrael during the interwar period and author of the work *Torat Avraham*. The Germans murdered Rabbi Grodzinski during the liquidation of the Kovno Ghetto.

Rabbi Chaim Leib Zacks (?- circa 1960). Rabbi of Uzdah and later a Rabbi at the yeshivah in Bailly or *Yeshivoth Reunis*. Rabbi Zacks was a decider of Jewish law. He ultimately moved to Cleveland with Leib and learned Talmud with him regularly. Rabbi Zaks was the father-in-law of the recently deceased Rosh Yeshivah in Telz, Rabbi Chaim Stein.

Rabbi Elchanan Wasserman (1874-1941). Rosh Yeshivah of *Ohel Torah* in Boronovich. Principal disciple of the the great Sage, Rabbi Yisrael Meir HaKohen, and author of *Kovetz Shiurim* (on the Talmud) and *Kovetz Maamarim* (on faith and thought). He was ultimately murdered at the Ninth Fort on July 7th, 1941, along with several well known Kovno Rabbis.

Rabbi Eliyahu-Meir Bloch (1895-1955). Along with his brother-in-law, Rabbi Chaim Mordechai Katz, he was the *Rosh Yeshivah* of the Telz Yeshivah in Cleveland.

Rabbi Isaac Elchanan Spektor (1817-1896). Community Rabbi in Kovno. Greatest *halakhist* of his generation, he decided Jewish law and resolved disputes for Jews around the world. During his tenure as Rabbi of Kovno, Kovno grew as a center for Torah study.

Rabbi Mordechai Pagramanski (1904-1949). Known as the Telzer Gaon (genius from Telz), he was a gifted Talmudic scholar in pre-Holocaust Lithuania. Rabbi Pagramanski ultimately lead Leib's yeshivah in Bailly, also called the Versaille Yeshivah, the *Yeshivoth Reunis*, or The Yeshivas Uniting the She'erith Hapleitah of Poland and Lithuania. Rabbi Pagramanski was a survivor of the Kovno ghetto.

Rabbi Meir. Sage after the destruction of the Jewish Temple in 70 CE. Though his opinion is usually not followed, his teachings are profound and constantly discussed and quoted in the Talmud. He was a student of Elisha ben Avuyah and Rabbi Akiva.

Rabbi Naftali Amsterdam (1832-1906). One of Rabbi Yisrael Salanter's main disciples. Well respected for his humility and piety, he was also a great Talmudist and proved to be of great influence to the Kovno religious community and select students at the Slobodka Yeshivah. Though preferring to be a private citizen, assisting his wife as a baker, Rabbi Amsterdam served in various Rabbinical posts including Rabbi in Helsinki, Saint Petersburg, and Alexot.

Rabbi Nathan Tzvi Finkel (1849-1927). Founder and *Mashgiach* of the Slobodka Yeshivah, *Knesset Yisrael*. The work *Ohr Hatzaphun* – "The Hidden Light" – records his teachings on ethics and *mussar*.

Rabbi Shnuer Zalman of Liadi (1745- 1812). Author of works on both *Kabbalah* and *halakha*, most notably the *Tanya* and the *Shulchan Aruch Ha'Rav*. Rabbi Shnuer Zalman was chosen to advocate the *Hasidic* cause in Lithuania. He was the founder of *Habad*.

Rabbi Yeffeh (?- circa 1941). Rabbi of Panemune.

Rabbi Yosef Chaim Zaks (1879-1941). Rosh Yeshivah of Slobodka's *Yeshivah Ketanah, Ohel Moshe*. Murdered at the Ninth Fort along with Rabbi Elchanan Wasserman.

Rabbi Yisrael Salanter (1810-1883). Great Talmudic scholar in nineteenth century Lithuania. Under the influence of Rabbi Zundel of Salant, Rabbi Yisrael Salanter lead and promoted the *mussar* movement. Emphasizing interpersonal ethics, character development, and conscious devotion to Torah and *mitzvot,* he and his followers strove to incorporate *mussar* and Jewish ethical literature into the yeshivah curriculum. His ideas had a tremendous influence on Lithuanian Jewry and yeshivah students until today. The yeshivah, *Knesset Yisrael*, is named after this great Sage.

Rabbi Yom Tov ben Avraham (circa 1260 – circa 1320). Spanish Medieval Rabbi famous for his commentary on the Talmud.

Rav Zalman Osowsky [or Osowski] (?-1941). Rabbi of Slobodka in the pre-Holocaust period.

Rochel Schames (circa 1924-1941). Leib's younger sister and twin sister of Dov Schames. She was murdered on the eighth of *Cheshvan* (October 29, 1941) along with her mother and siblings.

Ralph Kodikow [also spelled Codikow] (1930-circa 1995). Younger brother of Nathan Kodikow and resident of Panemune. A survivor of the Kovno Ghetto, Auschwitz, and Buchenwald, he reunited with Leib after the Holocaust in Los Angeles and ultimately became his close friend.

Sempo Sugihara (1900-1986). Japanese diplomat who served as Vice-Consul in Lithuania. He helped saved thousands of Jews, issuing transit visas so that they could emigrate to Japan safely before the Nazi onslaught.

Sturmfuehrer Jordan (?- circa 1942). German Commander of Ghetto Affairs in Kovno.

Vilna Gaon. See Gaon of Vilna

Wilhelm Goecke (1898-1944). S.S. Commander of the Mauthausen Concentration Camp and later head of the Kovno Concentration Camp.

Yitzhak Meir Schames also known as *Alter* ("Old man") Schames (1891-1941). Leib's father. He was murdered on the twelfth of *Tammuz* (July 7th, 1941) in the Seventh Fort.

Ze'ev Jabotinsky (1880-1940). Founder of the Zionist youth group, *Beitar*.

Notes

1 Before WWI, Lithuania was much larger than modern Lithuania today. Pre-WWI Lithuania (*Lita*), with its unique culture and perspective, consisted of modern day Lithuania, along with parts of Eastern Poland, Western Russian, Belarus and Latvia. Though Lithuania's borders shrunk after World War I, the Jewish population in parts of these areas can be thought of and in many cases, considered themselves, part of Lithuania and *Litvak* culture [Ozer, Mark N. *The Litvak Legacy*. Philadelphia: Xlibris, 2009, 25].

2 It should be noted that many of the stories recorded by my uncle, Mayer Schames, my grandfather repeated multiple times, to family members. My grandfather often revealed memories from different points in time and did not provide a chronological narrative. Though I source each episode to designate from whom I heard the story, these interviews sometimes confirmed the stories many in the family heard directly from my grandfather. Still, it must be mentioned that oral testimony, especially testimony given years after the Holocaust or passed down to children and grandchildren, is subject to inaccuracy. I have, therefore, reviewed multiple interviews, confirming stories between interviewees as well as compared these interviews with other testimonies and records in order to contextualize and detail much of my grandfather's oral testimony. The primary documents from the Diary of Avraham Tory, the anonymous members of the Jewish ghetto police, the memoirs of William Mishel, Rabbi Ephraim Oshry, Lazar Goldstein, Solly Ganor, Ralph Codikow, interviews from Judith Meisel, Dr. Jack Brauns and family, and Rabbi Pinchas Gruman, as well as documents from the German government, proved especially valuable. Furthermore, I have relied heavily on these primary sources to describe different experiences and episodes that occurred in the ghetto and the camps.

3 Joseph Schames, personal communication, 2007.

4 See *Iyov* 5:24.

5 See *Iyov* 42:12.

6 See *Iyov* 8:8.

7 *Vayikra* 10:3.

8 *Vayikra* 10:6.

9 Mayer Schames, personal communication, 2010; Leib Schames, personal communication, 2005. Chiene Schames (*nee* Feltenstein) came from a prestigious family. Her father had learned in the famous Telz Yeshivah, and Chiene herself was a righteous woman who possessed a profound yet simple faith in G-d [Leib Schames, personal communication, 2005].

10 Mayer Schames, personal communication, 2010 and 2016; Leib Schames, personal communication, 2005. Leib's father, Yitzhak Meir, was born in Lithuania. He learned in its famed yeshivah [religious school], *Knesset Yisrael*. In his early twenties, Yitzhak emigrated to the United States to find employment. Finding it difficult to work long hours and subsist on a few dollars, Yitzhak returned to his home country. Once back in Lithuania, Yitzhak was conscripted into the Russian army to fight in World War One. The young Yitzhak was eventually captured by the German army and spent the remainder of the war years as a prisoner in a German camp where he served as a translator. With the war over, Yitzhak moved to Kovno and married. He tried to manage the business some years back and was quite successful at one point in time. But, with the economic depression of the early 1930's, he left the business to his wife. He devoted his life to Talmudic study and writing a book of novel Torah insights [Mayer Schames, personal communication, 2010].

11 See Naftali Amsterdam, Halevanon, 15/37 (25 Apr. 1879), supplement, In Shaul Stampfer, *Lithuanian Yeshivas of the Nineteenth Century: Creating a Tradition of Learning*, Reprint Edition (Portland: Littman Library of Jewish Civilization, 2014), 266.

12 Leib Schames, Interview, 2002; Safira Rapoport, *A Pedigreed Jew: Between There and Here: Kovno and Israel*, trans. Pamela Hickman (Israel: Yad Vashem Pubns, 2010), 22; Rivka Wolbe, *Faith in the Night* (Brooklyn, N.Y.: Judaica Pr, 2009), 16; Dov Levin, "YIVO | Kaunas," n.d., http://www.yivoencyclopedia.org/article.aspx/Kaunas.

13 For views about Lithuanian Jewry and descriptions of their simplicity see Nathan Kamenetsky, *Making of a Godol: A Study of Episodes in the Lives of Great Torah Personalities, Improved Edition*, 2nd Revised edition (Jerusalem: pp, 2004), 602, Avraham Kariv, *Lithuania Land of My Birth* (Herzl Press, New York, 1967), 72; Abraham S. Sachs, *Worlds That Passed*, trans. H. Berman and J. Joffe (New York: Arno Press, 1975), 108-113 and 116-118; Rabbi Menachem Mendel Poliakoff, *Minhagei Lita: Customs of Lithuanian Jewry*, 56-76.

14 She would wait for them outside the House of Study, and when the Slobodka *Mashgiach* (spiritual dean), Rabbi Avraham Grodzinski, walked by, she quickly approached him to ask how her children were progressing in their studies [Leib Schames, Interview, 2002].

15 *Ohr Yisrael* had an enrollment of seventy to eighty boys between the ages of sixteen

and eighteen. The school for older children, *Knesset Yisrael*, had an enrollment of over three hundred students. And Leib's yeshivah, *Ohel Moshe*, had an enrollment of one hundred students between the ages of eleven and sixteen [R. Ephraim Oshry, *Annihilation of Lithuanian Jewry* (New York: Judaica Press, 1996), 10-11].

16 Stampfer, *Lithuanian Yeshivas of the Nineteenth Century*, 255.

17 Ozer, *The Litvak Legacy*, 34-35; Kamenetsky, *Making of a Godol*, 607.

18 See Gershon Movshovich, "The Old Man of Slobodka." In Lucy Dawidowicz, *The Golden Tradition: Jewish Life and Thought in Eastern Europe* (Syracuse, New York: 1st Syracuse University Press, 1996), 182.

19 See Gershon Movshovich, "The Old Man of Slobodka." In Dawidowicz, *The Golden Tradition: Jewish Life and Thought in Eastern Europe* , 182.

20 Lucy Dawidowicz, *The Golden Tradition: Jewish Life and Thought in Eastern Europe*, 180; See Marc Shapiro, *Between the Yeshiva World and Modern Orthodoxy: The Life and Works of Rabbi Jehiel Jacob Weinberg, 1884-1966* (Oxford; Portland, Or.: Littman Library of Jewish Civilization, 2002), 5-6.

21 See, for example, Samuel Schalkowsky trans, *The Clandestine History of the Kovno Jewish Ghetto Police*, (Bloomington: Indiana University Press, 2014), 359.

22 About three weeks before my grandfather's bar mitzvah, Chiene and Yitzhak Meir, due to a scheduling conflict, changed the *parshah* [the week's Torah portion] that Leib would need to read. Leib would have to learn an entirely different *parshah*, with the proper connotations and pronunciation, in two weeks. Leib learned the text quickly and on his bar mitzvah day, he read each verse correctly as if he had practiced it for the entire year [Henny Lent, Interview, 2012].

23 Leib Schames, Interview, 2005; Lazar Goldstein-Golden, *From Ghetto Kovno to Dachau* (Esther Goldstein, 1985), 30.

24 In the beginning of the twentieth century, participation in the agricultural industry declined and many gentiles competed with Jews as merchants [Ezra Mendelsohn, *The Jews of East Central Europe between the World Wars*, (Indiana University Press, 1987). 236-237].

25 c.f. *The Clandestine History of the Kovno Jewish Ghetto Police*, 228-229.

26 See Greenbaum, *The Jews of Lithuania*, 276.

27 Ibid. 279.

28 Bankier, David, and Ben-Tsiyon Klibansky. *Expulsion and Extermination: Holocaust Testimonials from Provincial Lithuania* (Jerusalem: Yad Vashem, the International Institute for Holocaust Research, 2011), 18; Karen Sutton, *The Massacre of the Jews of Lithuania* (Jerusalem: Gefen Publishing House, Ltd, 2008), 49-52.

29 Greenbaum, *The Jews of Lithuania*, 277.

30 Ibid, 278.

31 Rapoport, *A Pedigreed Jew: Between There and Here: Kovno and Israel*, 25-26.

32 Leib Schames, Interview 2005; During this interview, my grandfather informed me that the Panemune synagogue, though, continued to operate secretly for most, if not all of this time.

33 Mendelsohn, *The Jews of East Central Europe Between the World Wars*, 238; Leib Schames Interview 2005.

34 Leib Schames, Interview, 2005; Rapoport, *A Pedigreed Jew: Between There and Here: Kovno and Israel*, 31.

35 Leib Schames, Interview, 2005.

36 Rapoport, *A Pedigreed Jew: Between There and Here: Kovno and Israel*, 29; Greenbaum, *The Jews of Lithuania*, 293; Leib Schames, Interview, 2005.

37 Alexot is also known as Aleksotas and is referred to this in many maps.

38 In 1941, Vilna was incorporated into Russia and was not part of Lithuania.

39 Rabbi Osowsky was the chief Rabbi of the suburb of Slobodka.

40 My grandfather said in an interview that this was the Flack artillery building. [Leib Schames, recorded cassette interview, 1988].

41 This is not a literal number, as there were a few survivors from the Seventh Fort massacre, including my grandfather, his brother and his mother. My grandfather is trying to make a stylistic point and is not trying to give hard statistics.

42 *Berachos* 10a.

43 Based on my grandfather's birth certificate, he was actually eighteen at the time and his brother was sixteen. Throughout his life, my grandfather had trouble determining his exact age since he had altered it many times to show himself to be older or younger depending on circumstances in the ghetto or the camps. For the purposes of his story, I have kept his age, as he told it, throughout the book [Leib Schames, Birth Certificate; Mayer Schames, Interview, 2012].

44 According to Leib Schames's son, Mayer Schames, these documents were really his brother's old paperwork, not his own. Again, my grandfather, at this time, was eighteen and had no such paperwork testifying that he was fifteen [Mayer Schames, Interview, 2012].

45 My grandfather's best friend, Nathan Codikow, was murdered in the Seventh Fort as well, but he does not mention this in his memoir for some reason [*Lest We Forget*, 20].

46 Rabbi Elchanan Wasserman was part of the group whom my grandfather describes here. In Los Angeles, my grandfather told Rabbi Simcha Wasserman, Rabbi Elchanan Wasserman's son, that he made his father's *yahrzeit* [memorial for a relative that passed away] on a wrong day. However, Rabbi Simcha Wasserman felt that since he had kept a different *yahrzeit* for so long, it would not be right to change the day [Joseph Schames, Interview, 2012].

47 William W. Mishell, *Kaddish for Kovno: Life and Death in a Lithuanian Ghetto 1941-1945* (Chicago, Ill.: Chicago Review Press, 1999), 54; Oshry, *The Annihilation of Lithuanian Jewry*, 31; Diary of Elena Kutorgiene, August 12, 1941, *In the Hidden History of the Kovno Ghetto*, 50.

48 Mishell, *Kaddish for Kovno*, 54, 59; *The Clandestine History of the Jewish Ghetto Police*, 20, 73, 78.

49 Mishell, *Kaddish for Kovno*, 59.

50 See Instructions from Kovno's Lithuanian authorities to implement "Order No. 15," July 25, 1941. In *Hidden History of the Kovno Ghetto* (Boston: Bullfinch Press, 1997), 51.

51 Mayer Schames, Interview, June 12, 2011.

52 Interview with Lithuanian homeowner who currently owns the house, Summer 2004.

53 Mishell, *Kaddish for Kovno,* 66-67.

54 Oshry, *The Annihilation of Lithuanian Jewry*, 31.

55 Mayer Schames, Interview, June 12, 2011.

56 *See Mishell, Kaddish for Kovno,* 65; *The Clandestine History of the Jewish Ghetto Police*, 20.

57 *The Clandestine History of the Jewish Ghetto Police, 84; Mishell, Kaddish for Kovno,* 66-67.

58 Mishell, *Kaddish for Kovno*, 67; *The Clandestine History of the Jewish Ghetto Police*, 20.

59 Mayer Schames, Interview, June 12, 2011.

60 Ibid.

61 *The Clandestine History of the Jewish Ghetto Police*, 85-90; Mishell, *Kaddish for Kovno*, 69- 70, 39; Mayer Schames, Interview, June 12, 2011.

62 Mishell, *Kaddish for Kovno*, 94; See *The Clandestine History of the Jewish Ghetto Police*, 119.

63 *The Clandestine History of the Jewish Ghetto Police*, 106-112; Mishell, *Kaddish for Kovno*, 75-76. For example, Sturmfuehrer Jordan provided the Judenrat with over five thousand passes to be passed to artisans and trade specialists. These Jordan passes, as they were notoriously called, designated these people as useful and productive human beings protected from future *Aktions*.

64 William Mishell, *Kaddish for Kovno*, 81-82; Avraham Tory, *Surviving the Holocaust: The Kovno Ghetto Diary*, ed. Martin Gilbert and Dina Porat, trans. Jerzy Michalowicz (Harvard University Press, 1991), 38.

65 *Tanchuma Ki Tetze*, 13. *Pesikta de Rab Kahana, Piska* 3:10. *Pisikta Rabbati, Piska* 12:13. *Midrash HaGadol, Beshalach*, 17:8. In Elijah Schochet, *Amalek: the Enemy Within* (Mimetav Press, 1991), 41.

66 *Pirkei De-Rabbi Eliezer* , 44, 354-346. In Ibid.

67 *Tanchuma, Ki Tetze* 10. In Ibid; Ephraim Oshry, *Responsa from the Holocaust*, trans. Y. Leiman, Revised edition (New York: Judaica Press, 2001), xiv; Sol Littman, *War Criminal on Trial: Rauca of Kaunas* (Toronto: Key Porter Books, 1993), 83.

68 Mayer Schames, Interview, June 12, 2011. According to Mayer Schames, the Yom Kippur services might have actually taken place in the Schames's actual living quarters; See *The Clandestine History of the Jewish Ghetto Police*, 122-123.

69 Mishell, *Kaddish for Kovno*, 82.

70 *The Clandestine History of the Jewish Ghetto Police*, 125.

71 Oshry, *The Annihilation of Lithuanian Jewry*, 49; *The Clandestine History of the Jewish Ghetto Police*, 126; Rapoport, *A Pedigreed Jew: Between There and Here: Kovno and Israel*, 41.

72 Mishell, *Kaddish for Kovno*, 84; *The Clandestine History of the Jewish Ghetto Police*, 126. There were exceptions, where the young with work certificates went to the Fort, while at times, older men and women were allowed to live [*The Clandestine History of the Jewish Ghetto Police*, 126].

73 Mishell, *Kaddish for Kovno*, 84.

74 Ibid.

75 Oshry, *The Annihilation of Lithuanian Jewry*, 49.

76 Mishell, *Kaddish for Kovno*, 84.

77 Oshry, *The Annihilation of Lithuanian Jewry*, 48; Martin Gilbert, *Never Again: The History of the Holocaust* (Universe, 2000), 96.

78 *Kiddushin* 21b and Rashi ad loc.

79 Yitzhak Arad, *The "Final Solution" in Lithuania in the Light of German Documentation* (Yad Vashem, 1976), 249-250; Doris Bergen, *War and Genocide: A Concise History of the Holocaust*, 3 edition (Lanham: Rowman & Littlefield Publishers, 2016), 14.

80 Mishell, *Kaddish for Kovno*, 86.

81 Mishell, *Kaddish for Kovno*, 88; *The Clandestine History of the Jewish Ghetto Police*, 132, 134-135.

82 Oshry, *The Annihilation of Lithuanian Jewry*, 132; Mishell, *Kaddish for Kovno*, 88-89; Tory, *Surviving the Holocaust: The Kovno Ghetto Diary*, 47-48.

83 Oshry, *The Annihilation of Lithuanian Jewry*, 62.

84 Tory, *Surviving the Holocaust: The Kovno Ghetto Diary*, 50.

85 *Hidden History of the Kovno Ghetto*, 67; Oshry, *The Annihilation of Lithuanian Jewry*, 63; Mayer Schames, Interview, June 12, 2011.

86 *Hidden History of the Kovno Ghetto*, 67.

87 Mishell, *Kaddish for Kovno*, 91.

88 Leib Schames, Interview, October 11, 2003; Oshry, *The Annihilation of Lithuanian Jewry*, 63; Mishell, *Kaddish for Kovno*, 91; *The Clandestine History of the Jewish Ghetto Police*, 139.

89 Leib Schames, recorded cassette interview, 1988; Leib Schames, Conversation, October 11, 2003; Henny Lent, Interview, 2011; Esther Schames, Interview, 2011; Mayer Schames, Interview, June 12, 2011.

90 Esther Schames, Interview, 2012; Mayer Schames, Interview, June 12, 2011.

91 Mayer Schames, Interview, June 12, 2011; See *The Clandestine History of the Jewish Ghetto Police*, 141.

92 Oshry, *The Annihilation of Lithuanian Jewry*, 64; *Hidden History of the Kovno Ghetto*, 68.

93 Mishell, *Kaddish for Kovno*, 94.

94 Leib Schames, recorded cassette interview, 1988.

95 Mishell, *Kaddish for Kovno*, 94.

96 Ganor Solly, *Light One Candle: A Survivor's Tale from Lithuania to Jerusalem* (New York: Kodansha Amer Inc, 1995), 175-176; Mishell, *Kaddish for Kovno*, 94.

97 Vayikra 22:28

98 Leib Schames, recorded cassette interview, 1988.

99 Avraham Tory, *Surviving the Holocaust*, 55-58; *The Clandestine History of the Jewish Ghetto Police*, 143-147.

100 Leib Schames, "Dear Lithuanian Jews"; According to the Jaeger Report, 9,200 Jews were murdered on October 29, 1941 at the Ninth Fort. Though we can add the additional Jews who were murdered in the ghetto itself and died in Demacratu Plaza, it is difficult to understand how my grandfather's estimated 12,000 Jews. It is possible that he is adding the 2,000 Jews murdered in the Small Ghetto *Aktion* as well. I am unsure of this and have reported this number based on his estimation.

101 Mishell, *Kaddish for Kovno*, 94.

102 Leib Schames, recorded cassette interview, 1988; Henny Lent, Interview, 2011.

103 Leib Schames, recorded cassette interview, 1988.

104 Mishell, *Kaddish for Kovno*, 94-96.

105 Leib Schames, recorded cassette interview, 1988.

106 Avraham Tory, *Surviving the Holocaust*, 58; *The Clandestine History of the Jewish Ghetto Police*, 158-159; Mishell, *Kaddish for Kovno*, 96.

107 Ibid.

108 Mishell, *Kaddish for Kovno*, 100; Oshry, *Annihilation of Lithuanian Jewry*, 35; Gerber, *"Ilya Gerber: Kovno Ghetto."* In Alexandra Zapruder, *Salvaged Pages: Young Writers' Diaries of the Holocaust*, 352; The Germans provided working Jews with supplementary ration but, according to Mishel, even with this, the Jews could not survive [Mishell, *Kaddish for Kovno*, 100].

109 Goldstein-Golden, *From Ghetto Kovno to Dachau*, 32; *The Clandestine History of the Jewish Ghetto Police*, 150.

110 Goldstein-Golden, *From Ghetto Kovno to Dachau*, 32.

111 Avraham Tory, *Surviving the Holocaust*, 57; Rapoport, *A Pedigreed Jew: Between There and Here: Kovno and Israel*, 35; *The Clandestine History of the Jewish Ghetto Police*, 174.

112 Mishell, *Kaddish for Kovno*, 97; Rapoport, *A Pedigreed Jew: Between There and Here: Kovno and Israel*, 35; See also *The Clandestine History of the Jewish Ghetto Police*, 104-105 for descriptions of trading before the *Grosse Aktion*.

113 See Oshry, *Responsa from the Holocaust* where he, in fact, encouraged the practice of taking a dead person's clothing for trade.

114 Leib Schames, recorded cassette interview, 1988; Mayer Schames, Interview, June 12, 2011; See *The Clandestine History of the Jewish Ghetto Police*, 260-262.

115 Judith Meisel, Interview, 2011; See *The Clandestine History of the Jewish Ghetto*

Police, 174; Mayer Schames, Interview, June 12, 2011; Mayer Schames said: "Motke had been an orphan – a *yatom* - for most of his life. He knew how to fend for himself and how to manage resources. Now, after the *Grosse Aktion*, Motke the *yatom* took in Leible the *yatom* [Mayer Schames, Interview, 2012]."

116 Mayer Schames, Interview, 2012; See Gerber, *"Ilya Gerber: Kovno Ghetto."* In Alexandra Zapruder, *Salvaged Pages: Young Writers' Diaries of the Holocaust,* 339. c.f *The Clandestine History of the Jewish Ghetto Police*, 168. My grandfather did not mention when he switched from the *Flugplatz* to the roofer brigade or if he switched back. Additionally, I have assumed that he, most likely, was able to switch with the help of Motke who had pull with the authorities.

117 Mayer Schames, Interview, June 12, 2011; See Gerber, *"Ilya Gerber: Kovno Ghetto."* In Alexandra Zapruder, *Salvaged Pages: Young Writers' Diaries of the Holocaust,* 352

118 Mayer Schames, Interview, June 12, 2011.

119 Gerber, *"Ilya Gerber: Kovno Ghetto."* In Alexandra Zapruder, *Salvaged Pages: Young Writers' Diaries of the Holocaust,* 336; *The Clandestine History of the Jewish Ghetto Police*, 320. See Avraham Tory, *Surviving the Holocaust*, 115, where he explains that between late July and August 1942, the Germans left the responsibility for inspections completely with the Lithuanians guards. The Germans oversaw work and production, but they negligently monitored the Jews as they came back into the ghetto. The Nazi foremen did not confiscate any goods or show interest in reprimanding smugglers. The Lithuanians guards at the checkpoint followed suit and for the next few weeks, the Lithuanian guards apathetically allowed goods to pass into the ghetto. In return, the food supply in the ghetto increased and the price of butter, potatoes, and meats depreciated.

120 Gerber,*"Ilya Gerber: Kovno Ghetto."* In Alexandra Zapruder, *Salvaged Pages: Young Writers' Diaries of the Holocaust,* 336.

121 Ibid; See *The Clandestine History of the Jewish Ghetto Police*, 266-267.

122 See Gerber,*"Ilya Gerber: Kovno Ghetto."* In Alexandra Zapruder, *Salvaged Pages: Young Writers' Diaries of the Holocaust,* 354.

123 See Ibid., 354 and *The Clandestine History of the Jewish Ghetto Police*, 321.

124 Gerber,*"Ilya Gerber: Kovno Ghetto."* In Alexandra Zapruder, *Salvaged Pages: Young Writers' Diaries of the Holocaust,* 354-355; c.f *The Clandestine History of the Jewish Ghetto Police*, 263-264, 274.

125 The song was written in September 1941 by Avrom Akselrod, a resident of the Kovno Ghetto. My grandfather explained that these songs allowed those who didn't experience the Shoah to picture what the experience was like [Leib Schames, recorded cassette interview, 1988].

126 This refers to the Jewish police who patrolled the gate and wore an armband with a red stripe.

127 Leib Schames, recorded cassette interview, 1988; My grandfather only repeated the first portion of the song until "He grabs it from your hands."

128 Leib Schames, recorded cassette interview, 1988.

129 Waldemar Ginsberg, *And Kovno Wept* (Laxon, Newark, Nottinghamshire: The Holocaust Centre, 1998), 70; Gerber, "*Ilya Gerber: Kovno Ghetto.*" In Alexandra Zapruder, *Salvaged Pages: Young Writers' Diaries of the Holocaust,* 352-354; *The Clandestine History of the Jewish Ghetto Police*, 176, 260.

130 Leib Schames, recorded cassette interview, 1988.

131 Leib Schames, recorded cassette interview, 1988.

132 Ralph Codikow, recorded cassette interview, 1988; See *The Clandestine History of the Jewish Ghetto Police*, 264-265.

133 Mayer Schames, Interview, June 12, 2011; See *The Clandestine History of the Jewish Ghetto Police*, 255-262.

134 Mayer Schames, Interview, 2011.

135 Leib Schames, Cassette Interview, 1988.

136 Judith Meisel, Interview, 2011.

137 See Gerber, "*Ilya Gerber: Kovno Ghetto.*" In Alexandra Zapruder, *Salvaged Pages: Young Writers' Diaries of the Holocaust,* 352; *Hidden History of the Kovno Ghetto*, 136; Judith Meisel, Interview, 2011; *The Clandestine History of the Jewish Ghetto Police*, 174.

138 Mayer Schames, Interview 2011; Only a few months prior, on June 29, 1942, Lithuanian partisan murdered three Jews in their sleep at Palemonas. See Avraham Tory, *Surviving the Holocaust: The Kovno Ghetto Diary*, 100.

139 Mayer Schames, Interview, 2011; Gerber, "*Ilya Gerber: Kovno Ghetto.*" In Alexandra Zapruder, *Salvaged Pages: Young Writers' Diaries of the Holocaust,* 346.

140 See Gerber, "*Ilya Gerber: Kovno Ghetto.*" In Alexandra Zapruder, *Salvaged Pages: Young Writers' Diaries of the Holocaust,* 346.

141 See Ibid., 358-359 and *The Clandestine History of the Jewish Ghetto Police*, 322.

142 See Gerber, "*Ilya Gerber: Kovno Ghetto.*" In Alexandra Zapruder, *Salvaged Pages: Young Writers' Diaries of the Holocaust,* 346, 358.

143 Mayer Schames, Interview, 2011; This was a common occurrence and made filling the quota last days longer than expected [*The Clandestine History of the Jewish Ghetto Police*, 322].

144 Mayer Schames, Interview, 2011.

145 Leib Schames quoted in the name of Mayer Schames [Mayer Schames, Interview, June 12, 2011].

146 Levin, "How the Jewish Police in the Kovno Ghetto Saw Itself," 31.

147 Leib Schames, Cassette Interview, 1988; Mayer Schames, Interview, June 12, 2011; See Rapoport, *A Pedigreed Jew: Between There and Here: Kovno and Israel*, 45; Goldstein-Golden, *From Ghetto Kovno to Dachau*, 32; *The Clandestine History of the Jewish Ghetto Police,* 114, 162-163, 266.

148 Mayer Schames, Interview, 2012.

149 Leib Schames, Cassette Interview, 1988.

150 Rapoport, *A Pedigreed Jew: Between There and Here: Kovno and Israel*, 46; Mayer

Schames, Interview, 2012; Leib Schames, Cassette Interview, 1988.

151 Tory, *Surviving the Holocaust*, 189-193; Ginsberg, *And Kovno Wept*, 70.

152 Ibid., 194 -195; Apparently this was "revenge" for the German loss at Stalingrad, as if Jews somehow were responsible for this defeat [See *The Clandestine History of the Jewish Ghetto Police*, 293].

153 Tory, *Surviving the Holocaust*, 194 -195.

154 Ginsberg, *And Kovno Wept*, 70.

155 See Tory, *Surviving the Holocaust*, 195.

156 Samuel Gringauz, *"The Ghetto as an Experiment of Jewish Social Organization (Three Years of Kovno Ghetto),"* *Jewish Social Studies*, 11, 1 (1949), *3 -20;* Oshry, *Annihilation of Lithuanian Jewry*, 104.

157 Mishell, *Kaddish for Kovno*, 161.

158 Oshry, *Annihilation of Lithuanian Jewry*, 104.

159 Mishell, *Kaddish for Kovno*, 163.

160 Ibid.

161 Ibid., 164.

162 Ibid.

163 See Ibid., 166.

164 Ibid.

165 Mayer Schames, Interview, 2011.

166 Leib planned to escape with a friend from his brigade. The two planned to smuggle a gun from the partisans and murder the Lithuanian foreman on the way to the worksite. They would then escape to the partisans. His comrade smuggled the gun into the ghetto. Both men were ready to carry out the act. But on the day of their planned escape, Leib's friend lost his nerve [Mayer Schames, interview 2011]. This story probably took place at this time, before his time in the sub-camp at Alexot. It most likely did not happen earlier since the risks outweighed the benefits during the early part of the "quiet years" as escaped Jews were easily identified. Most Jews were brunette. Many gentiles were blond. Unlike Lithuanians, male Jews were circumcised. Describing the differences between Jews and gentiles in Lithuania, Ralph Codikow asked, "Can a black man pretend to be white? [Ralph Codikow, Cassset Interview, 1988]." Yet, at this stage in ghetto, with the upcoming creation of the Kovno Concentration Camp, the benefits to escaping outweighed the risks.

167 See Sachs, *Words that Passed*, 156.

168 Simchat Torah services.

169 See Rabbi Joseph B. Soloveitchik, *Halakhic Man* (The Jewish Publication Society, 1984), 77; Rabbi Yisrael Meir Ha'Kohen, *Mishnah Berurah*, 669:1 note 11.

170 Henny Lent, Interview, 2011; I am unsure exactly when this story took place. Based on the context, this most likely took place during this period when there were more religious and cultural freedoms. The Germans were relatively tolerant of religion during this period as they were occupied with completing the liquidation

of the Vilna Ghetto [*Kaddish for Kovno*, 166]. There is a possibility, though, that this story occurred during Simchat Torah of 1941. But, I believe, that it more likely took place at this time. See Oshry, *Annihilation of Lithuanian Jewry*, 75, who writes that although the Nazis took away their religious books about a year and a half before, the Jews managed to hide some Torah scrolls in a barn behind a wall.

171 Pinchas Gruman, Interview, January, 2013 quoting Rabbi Mordechai Pagramanski, the great Lithuanian Talmudic scholar and survivor of the Kovno Ghetto.

172 The Ukrainian men were defectors from the Red Army.

173 Mishell, *Kaddish for Kovno*, 167-172.

174 Leib Schames recorded cassette interview 1988, quoting a ghetto poem about the Ninth Fort written by an unknown ghetto resident, his comments are in parenthesis. My grandfather concluded: "You see, everything was true but the last part was not true, we never took any *nekamah* (revenge)."

175 See Tory, *Surviving the Holocaust*, 511.

176 They later made Block B into S.S. headquarters.

177 Mishell, *Kaddish for Kovno*, 179.

178 Ibid.

179 Ibid.

180 Tory, *Surviving the Holocaust*, 481.

181 Arad, *The Final Solution in Lithuania in Light of German Documentation*, 265.

182 Ibid., 179

183 I know based on his testimony that my grandfather spent six months in the concentration camp in Alexot (from late February to late July 1944). Yet, I am not completely sure where he worked or how he lived from late November 1943 until February 1944. I assumed that like many people in the ghetto, he tried to avoid the camps and perform labor within the ghetto fence. He probably also did this so that it would be easier for him to trade. He also could have done this because those who worked in the ghetto workshops were thought to be protected from future *Aktions* since ghetto workers avoided later deportations. This is assumed by this author, not based on testimony [See Mishell, *Kaddish for Kovno*, 180].

184 Judith Meisel, Interview, 2011.

185 Ibid.

186 Ibid.

187 Ibid.; Mayer Schames, Interview, 2011. A few months later, the Germans transported Motke to Dachau. Motke survived the war and later moved to the Land of Israel, residing there for a few years before passing away from heart failure [Mayer Schames, Interview, 2011].

188 Mishell, *Kaddish for Kovno*, 204.

189 Leib Schames, Cassette Interview 1988; Oshry, *Annihilation of Lithuanian Jewry*, 122.

190 Mishell, *Kaddish for Kovno*, 207.

191 Ibid.; Oshry, *Annihilation of Lithuanian Jewry*, 121-130.

192 Oshry, *Annihilation of Lithuanian Jewry*, 122-123; Robert Hillard, *Surviving the Americans: The Continued Struggle of the Jews After Liberation* (Seven Stories Press, 1996), 18.

193 See Yirmiyahu 6:25.

194 See Mishell, *Kaddish for Kovno*, 208.

195 Ibid.

196 See Ruth 1:16-17; Oshry, *Annihilation of Lithuanian Jewry*, 123-124.

197 Leib Schames, Cassette Interview, 1988; Mishell, *Kaddish for Kovno*, 208; Oshry, *Annihilation of Lithuanian Jewry*, 125.

198 Leib Schames, Cassette Interview, 1988.

199 Leib Schames, Cassette Interview, 1988.

200 Oshry, *Annihilation of Lithuanian Jewry*, 124-125; Many were also murdered before being taking to the train. According to Professor Samuel Kassow, this second group was taken away and murdered at the Ninth Fort [*The Clandestine History of the Kovno Jewish Ghetto Police*, 3].

201 Mishell, *Kaddish for Kovno*, 211-217.

202 Ginsberg, *And Kovno Wept*, 89-90.

203 Ibid., 90.

204 Oshry, *Annihilation of Lithuanian Jewry*, 125; *The Clandestine History of the Kovno Jewish Ghetto Police*, xv, 3; Mishell, *Kaddish for Kovno*, 217. Mishell mentions that of these two thousand people, over a thousand children were taken that day.

205 See Oshry, *Annihilation of Lithuanian Jewry*, 134.

206 Oshry, *Annihilation of Lithuanian Jewry*, 139; I realize that according to the previous calculations, the number of Jews who were in Kovno now should be less than fourteen thousand. These are all estimates provided by Rabbi Ephraim Oshry. These numbers should be taken as estimates and not hard statistics.

207 Leib Schames, recorded cassette interview 1988.

208 If he stayed in Kovno for another week, the Russian army would have liberated him [Mayer Schames, Interview, 2011]; *The Hidden History of the Kovno Ghetto*, 249.

209 See Mishell, *Kaddish for Kovno*, 275; Leib Schames, Interview, 2005.

210 Ibid., 279-280.

211 Ibid., 282.

212 Ibid., 279-283.

213 This date is based on my grandfather testimony of having only spent a night in Stuthoff and having entered Kaufering three days later on July 29, 1944 [Manfred Kesting, Summary of Findings from International Tracing Service, Germany, February 7, 2011].

214 Mishell, *Kaddish for Kovno*, 283-284.

215 See Ibid., 284-286.

216 See Ibid., 287.

217 Ibid.

218 Leib Schames, recorded cassette interview. 1988; Mishell, *Kaddish for Kovno*, 288.

219 Leib Schames, recorded cassette interview, 1988.

220 "We didn't have a chance to take anything out [Leib Schames, recorded cassette interview, 1988]."

221 Leib said, "Someone that knew *davening* by heart could have prayed. But, things like matzah in the camps was impossible [Leib Schames, recorded cassette interview, 1988]."

222 In a conversation with Ralph Codikow, a survivor of Birkanau, Ralph informed my grandfather that there was some sort of gathering of ten men for prayer [a *minyan*] in his camp. My grandfather responded immediately, "Not in my place." According to my grandfather, religious practice in places like Auschwitz-Birkanau was mostly performed by Hungarian Jews who only experienced German rule for eight to nine months at the end of 1944. In his view, they were shipped to Auschwitz still filled with the "same spirit and belief that they would be saved." However, for a Lithuanian survivor who experienced three years of *Aktions*, murder and slave labor in the Kovno ghetto, practicing Judaism was inappropriate [Ralph Codikow and Leib Schames, recorded cassette interview, 1988].

223 According to testimony from Henny Lent, Leib said to her that "the shirt seemed like it was moving" from the lice [Henny Lent, Interview 2011]. See Mishell, *Kaddish for Kovno*, 290-291.

224 Leib Schames, recorded cassette interview 1988.

225 Judith Meisel, Interview, 2011.

226 Leib Schames, later writings.

227 Mishell, *Kaddish for Kovno*, 292-293; Goldstein-Golden, *From Ghetto Kovno to Dachau*, 73.

228 Leib Schames's Prisoner's Personal Sheet of the Concentration Camp Dachau (7.29.44), Doc. No. 10283989#1(1.1.6.2/SCHAJC-SCHEK/00086194/0002) in conformity with International Tracing Service Archives, Germany.

229 Kaufering I was one of eleven sub-camps in Dachau (Kaufering I through XI). I know based on records and primary sources that many Kovno prisoners were transferred at this time to Kaufering I. My grandfather, though, did not mention which Kaufering camp he stayed in. I have assumed the he was in Kaufering I based on survivor testimony, records of numbers and other details mentioned by my grandfather.

230 Mishell, *Kaddish for Kovno*, 296.

231 Ibid.

232 Solly Ganor, "A Journey to the Past: Kaddish for Zelig," July 25, 2006, http://www.buffalo-israellink. org/IsraelStory2.htm; Jack Brauns, *Recollections and Reflections: How I Turned Despair into an Appreciation of Life* (Vallentine Mitchell, 2007),

84-88; Ginsberg, *And Kovno Wept*. 100, 105; Paul Berben, *Dachau, 1933-45: The Official History* (London: Norfolk Press, 1975), 77.

233 Mayer Schames, Interview, 2011, 2016; Mishell, *Kaddish for Kovno*, 299; Berben, *Dachau, 1933-45*, 76. According to Mayer Schames Interview 2011 and 2016, Moll was also associated with Phillip Holzmann. However, see Manfred Deiler, *The War Factory Project "Ringeltaube"* at <http://www.buergervereinigung-landsberg.org/english/historicalfacts/history.htm> who states that there were three separate companies – Leonhard Moll company, Phillip Holzmann and the Karl Stohr construction firm – each responsible for three different bunkers and who each procured Jewish slave labor from Kaufering.

234 See Ladislaus Ervin-Deutsch, "About Those Who Survived and Those who Died." *Dachau Review: History of Nazi Concentration Camps Studies*, 1 (2002): 146.

235 Ladislaus Ervin-Deutsch, "About Those Who Survived and Those who Died." *Dachau Review: History of Nazi Concentration Camps Studies*, 1 (2002): 140; See Selmond Greenberg testimony in Manfred Deiler, *The War Factory Project "Ringeltaube"* at <http://www.buergervereinigung-landsberg.org/english/historicalfacts/history.htm>

236 Ginsberg, *And Kovno Wept*, 104.

237 Berger, *No Time for Patience*, 74.

238 Ganor, "A Journey to the Past: Kaddish for Zelig."

239 Mayer Schames, Interview, 2011; See Ganor, "A Journey to the Past: Kaddish for Zelig." Mayer Schames, Interview, 2011; Miroslav Karny, Testimony. In Manfred Deiler, ed, Landsberg *Im 20. Jahrhundert: Contemporary Witnesses Describe the Hell of Kaufering*, accessed March 14, 2016, http://www.buergervereinigung-landsberg.org/english/historicalfacts/stories.htm.

240 Mishell, *Kaddish for Kovno*, 299.

241 Ibid.

242 Goldstein-Golden, *From Ghetto Kovno to Dachau*, 79.

243 Selmond Greenberg testimony in Manfred Deiler, *The War Factory Project "Ringeltaube"* at <http://www.buergervereinigung-landsberg.org/english/historicalfacts/history.htm>

244 See Baba Batra 8b; See Ganor, "A Journey to the Past: Kaddish for Zelig," July 25, 2006, http://www.buffalo-israellink. org/IsraelStory2.htm; Berben, *Dachau: 1933-45*, 89.

245 Leib Schames's Prisoner's Personal Sheet of the Concentration Camp Dachau (7.29.44), Doc. No. 10283989#1(1.1.6.2/SCHAJC-SCHEK/00086194/0002) in conformity with International Tracing Service Archives, Germany.

246 Gerber, *"Ilya Gerber: Kovno Ghetto."* In *Salvaged Pages: Young Writers' Diaries of the Holocaust, Second Edition:* Alexandra Zapruder, 360; *The Clandestine History of the Jewish Ghetto Police*, 276.

247 Zev Birger, *No Time for Patience: My Road from Kaunas to Jerusalem* (New York: William Morrow, 1999), 74; Ginsberg, *And Kovno Wept*, 105; Mayer Schames,

Interview 2011; The iron bars were then transported by train to a designated area where they were used as pins to stabilize the concrete arch.

248 Leib Schames Dachau Concetration Camp Card (8.1.44), Doc. No. 10744744#1(1.1.6.7/SARL-SCHEE/1138) in conformity with International Tracing Service Archives, Germany; Ginsberg, *And Kovno Wept*, 99,101; Mishell, *Kaddish for Kovno*, 302-303.

249 Mayer Schames Interview, 2012.

250 Mayer Schames, Interview, 2012; This hole was made by another prisoner who was probably trying to get to the tubers as well [Mayer Schames, Interview, 2012].

251 Mayer Schames, Interview, 2011.

252 Leib Schames, recorded cassette interview, 1988; Mayer Schames Interview, 2012.

253 Ibid.

254 Ibid.

255 Leib Schames, recorded cassette interview, 1988.

256 Esther Schames, Interview, 2011.

257 Ibid.

258 Mayer Schames, Interview, 2012; Leib Schames, personal communication, 2003.

259 c.f. Avot 4:1.

260 Leib Schames, "The Children of Israel Should Cry Over the Fire which Hashem Burnt," (Unpublished Essay, September 2, 1947).

261 Mayer Schames, Interview 2011; Esther Schames, Interview, 2011; See Levi, *Survival in Auschwitz*, 34-35.

262 Ginsberg, *And Kovno Wept*,104; Mishell, *Kaddish for Kovno*, 302-303; Berben, *Dachau, 1933-45,* 78; Mayer Schames, Interview, 2011; Manfred Deiler, ed, "Landsberg Im 20. Jahrhundert: Contemporary Witnesses Describe the Hell of Kaufering," accessed March 14, 2016, http://www.buergervereinigung-landsberg.org/english/historicalfacts/stories.htm.

263 Mayer Schames, Interview 2011; Ginsberg, *And Kovno Wept*, 103-104. It should be noted that the punishment for taking German goods was often death.

264 Mishell, *Kaddish for Kovno*, 306; Mayer Schames, Interview, 2011; *Yirmeyahu*, 9:21; See Sam Berger, Testimony. In Manfred Deiler, ed, "Landsberg Im 20. Jahrhundert: Contemporary Witnesses Describe the Hell of Kaufering," accessed March 14, 2016, http://www.buergervereinigung-landsberg.org/english/historicalfacts/stories.htm.

265 Ginsberg, *And Kovno Wept*, 102.

266 Mayer Schames, Interview, 2011.

267 Mayer Schames, Interview, 2011; See Thomas Madle, Testimony. In Manfred Deiler, ed, "Landsberg Im 20. Jahrhundert: Contemporary Witnesses Describe the Hell of Kaufering," accessed March 14, 2016, http://www.buergervereinigung-landsberg.org/english/historicalfacts/stories.htm.

268 Leib also randomly found a burnt $100 bill [Mayer Schames, Interview, 2011].

269 Leib Schames, recorded cassette interview, 1988.

270 Mayer Schames, Interview, 2011.

271 Ginsberg, *And Kovno Wept*, 106.

272 Ibid., 107; Mayer Schames, Interview, 2011.

273 Mayer Schames, Interview, 2011.

274 Leib Schames, personal communication, 2003; Henny Lent, Interview, 2005.

275 Ginsberg, *And Kovno Wept*, 106.

276 See *Shir Ha'Shirim* 8:7.

277 *Kiddushin* 39b.

278 *Menachos* 43b.

279 Leib Schames, "*Parshat Shelach*" (Unpublished Essay, Based on Interview with Joseph Schames, 2012).

280 Kings II 2:14.

281 Mayer Schames, Interview, 2011; Esther Schames, Interview, 2012.

282 Leib Schames, personal communication, 2003.

283 Ginsberg, *And Kovno Wept*, 112.

284 Ginsberg, *And Kovno Wept*, 113-114.

285 Mayer Schames, Interview, 2011.

286 Warren Lent, Interview, 2011.

287 Ibid.

288 Warren Lent, Interview, 2011; Mayer Schames, Interview, 2011.

289 Warren Lent, Interview, 2011; Mayer Schames, Interview, 2011.

290 In the morning, Leib heard two Ukrainians sitting on the ground talking to one another. Fearful of Ukrainians who helped carry out the *Kinder Aktion* and participated in other ghetto pogroms, Leib asked the farmer if he could live in his home and the man obliged [Mayer Schames, Interview, 2011].

291 Mayer Schames, Interview, 2011; Esther Schames, Interview, 2011; Henny Lent, Interview, 2011.

292 See *Tehillim* 12:9; *Tehillim* 11:3.

293 *Baba Metzia* 59a.

294 Leib Schames, "The Children of Israel should Cry Over the Fire which Hashem Burnt."

295 Leib Schames, recorded cassette interview, 1988.

296 Leib Schames, "Nekamah" (Unpublished Essay, unknown date); See *Bereshit* 4:10.

297 Mishell, *Kaddish for Kovno*, 350.

298 Hillard, *Surviving the Americans: The Continued Struggle of the Jews After Liberation*, 25-26, 45.

299 Leib Schames' St. Ottilien Medical Records, Doc. No. 79690566#2(3.2.1.1/S01366-01430/S01386/0002) in conformity with International Tracing Service Archives,

Germany; Hillard, *Surviving the Americans: The Continued Struggle of the Jews After Liberation*, 49-54; Mayer Schames, Interview, 2011.

300 Joseph Schames, Interview, 2012; See Hillard, *Surviving the Americans: The Continued Struggle of the Jews After Liberation*, 157. From Hilliard's words this story must have happened after September 1945, when the barbed wire fence was removed and St. Ottilion posted Jewish sentries, instead of American police units.

301 Zeev W. Mankowitz, *Life between Memory and Hope: The Survivors of the Holocaust in Occupied Germany* (New York: Cambridge University Press, 2002), 30; Mayer Schames, Interview, 2011.

302 Esther Schames, Interview, 201.

303 Mankowitz, *Life between Memory and Hope*, 235-239, c.f 246-247.

304 Leib Schames's St. Ottilien Medical Records, Doc. No. 79690566#2(3.2.1.1/S01366-01430/S01386/0002) in conformity with International Tracing Service Archives, Germany.

305 Ibid.

306 Ibid.

307 Mayer Schames, Interview, 2011 .

308 Manfred Kesting, Summary of Findings from International Tracing Service, Germany, February 7, 2011; Mankowitz, *Life between Memory and Hope*, 271.

309 Manfred Kesting, Summary of Findings from International Tracing Service, Germany, February 7, 2011.

310 Ibid.; Mayer Schames, Interview, 2011.

311 Leib Schames, personal communication, 2006.

312 Mayer Schames, Interview, 2011 .

313 Pinchas Gruman, Interview, 2013.

314 Ibid.

315 The yeshivah was orginally formed in Prague and moved to Bailly.

316 Pinchas Gruman, Interview, 2013.

317 Oshry, *Annihilation of Lithuanian Jewry*, 132-133.

318 Pinchas Gruman, Interview, 2013; Yossi Schames, Interview, 2012; Oshry, *Annihilation of Lithuanian Jewry,*133.

319 Yossi Schames, Interview, 2012.

320 At his *Sheva Berachos* [one of Seven Festive meals following his wedding], Rabbi Pagramanski presented the outlines to Darwin's theory of evolution and explained how the theory possessed many intellectual holes."Why," he asked, "did the Western World so readily accept the theory?" Reminiscent of the Talmud's statement on idol worship, Rabbi Pagramanski explained that a person who wants to behave like an animal will try to rationalize and accept any theory. He will accept a theory like evolution if he believes (at least on a subconcious level) that he is an animal [Pinchas Gruman, Interview, 2013]. It should be noted that my grandfather took a more moderate position when dealing with such matters. When asked whether

one is allowed to attend a class which taught evolution, my grandfather said that such a thing was permitted. He said that even if evolution is correct, one must ask the question of where did original matter come from. "Only G-d can create something from nothing," he explained, "something cannot come from nothing." My grandfather did not necessarily subscribe to evolution, rather believing that the theory did not contradict Torah [Leib Schames, personal communication, 2006]. Lithuanian Rabbis such as Rabbi Elchanan Wasserman, Rabbi Avraham Isaac Kook, and Rabbi Boruch Ber Leibovitz took various approaches when dealing with this question.

321 Oshry, *Annihilation of Lithuanian Jewry,* 133.

322 Esther Schames, Interview, 2012; Rabbi Zaks was the father-in-law of the recently deceased Rosh Yeshivah in Telz, Rabbi Chaim Stein.

323 See Yechiel Yaakov Weinberg, *"The Mussar Movement." In Men of the Spirit*, ed. Leo Jung, (Kymson Publishing Company, 1964), 252.

324 Yitchak encouraged Leib to become a *schochet.*

325 Leib Schames, Interview, 1988.

326 *Iyov* 4:7.

327 Leib Schames, recorded cassette interview, 1988.

328 Greenbaum, *The Jews of Lithuania,* 345; Some estimate a little more - almost 96% of pre-Holocaust Lithuanian Jewry, some a little less - 90% of pre-Holocaust Lithuanian Jewry [Ozer, *The Litvak Legacy*, 90].

329 Ozer, *The Litvak Legacy*, 90.

330 Joseph Schames, personal communication, 2007.

331 cf. Devarim 25:17-19.

332 Leib Schames, "Nekamah" (Unpublished Essay, unknown date).

333 See Leib Schames, "Lecture on Parshat Pinchas" (Unpublished Essay, July 9, 1947). See Zalman Grinberg's June 10, 1945 speech at https://www.jewishvirtuallibrary.org/jsource/Holocaust/GrinbergSpeech.html; See Mankowitz, *Life between Memory and Hope*, 235-240.

334 Manfred Kesting, Summary of Findings from International Tracing Service, Germany, February 7, 2011.

335 Esther Schames, Interview, 2012.

336 Leib Schames, recorded cassette interview, 1988.

337 *Iyov* 8:7; 5:24.

338 At the time of his death in 2007, he had twelve grandchildren and one great grandchild. My grandmother was interviewed by the Shoah Foundation in 1997. At the end of this interview, my grandfather came into the room and was asked to speak. The following are his words: "Coming after the big tragedy that we went through in the Holocaust, we have to thank G-d, first, for G-d gives life. Second, [we have to thank G-d] for what life can produce after what we went through. Thank G-d, I have two sons and a daughter...Thank G-d we have twelve grandchildren. Thank G-d, He gave us the opportunity to continue the family, progressing for a

good and honorable life, for the Jewish people and people in the United States" [Esther and Leib Schames, Shoah Foundation Interview, 1997].

339 See *Iyov* 5:24-25.

340 See *Iyov* 8:8.

341 *Vayikra* 10:3.

342 *Vayikra* 10:6.

343 *Eichah* 1:1.

344 *Bereshit Rabbah* 19:9.

345 *Bereshit* 3:9.

346 They are both spelled with the same Hebrew letters, though they are vowelized differently.

347 In other words, I would like to express mourning [*Eichah*] with the word "where" [*Ayyekkah*].

348 In November 1943, sixty-four Jews were forced by the Gestapo to open the pits and incinerate the bodies around Fort Nine.

349 *Eichah* 2:13.

350 See *Bereshit* 32:9; See *Ezekiel* 37:2; See *Zechariah* 3:2.